DATE DUE

P9-CKO-614

WORKING WITH FACULTY TO DESIGN UNDERGRADUATE INFORMATION LITERACY PROGRAMS

A How-To-Do-It Manual for Librarians

Rosemary M. Young
and
Stephena Harmony

HOW-TO-DO-IT MANUALS FOR LIBRARIANS

NUMBER 90

NEAL-SCHUMAN PUBLISHERS, INC.
New York, London

Riverside Community College
'99   Library
OCT   4800 Magnolia Avenue
Riverside, CA 92506

Z 711.2 .Y68 1999

Young, Rosemary, 1950-

Working with faculty to
design undergraduate

All handouts and worksheets created by the authors.
Reprinted with permission.

The graphics in Chapter 7 are from the Raymond Walters College Library's
Web page (www.rwc.uc.edu/library/) and reprinted with permission.

Published by Neal-Schuman Publishers, Inc.
100 Varick Street
New York, NY 10013

Copyright © 1999 Rosemary M. Young and Stephena Harmony

All rights reserved. Reproduction of this book, in whole or in part, without
written permission of the publisher, is prohibited.

Printed and bound in the United States of America.

Library of Congress Cataloging-in-Publication Data

Young, Rosemary, 1950–
      Working with faculty to design undergraduate information literacy
programs / Rosemary M. Young, Stephena Harmony.
          p. cm. — (How-to-do-it manuals for librarians ; no. 90)
      Includes bibliographical references and index.
      ISBN 1-55570-354-2
      1. Library orientation for college students—United States.
   2. Information retrieval—Study and teaching (Higher)—United
States.   I. Harmony, Stephena.   II. Title.   III. Series: How-to-do-
it manuals for libraries ; no. 90.
   Z711.2.Y68   1999
   027.7'0973—dc21   98-54783
                                                              CIP

CONTENTS

FIGURES

PREFACE

Creating an information literacy program from scratch is a daunting task. We became acutely aware of this when, as colleagues in branch campus libraries of a large urban university, we began teaching undergraduates the fundamentals of information literacy. As we compared notes, shared successful strategies, and commiserated over frustrating moments, we began to realize that we needed to synthesize our discoveries—both the philosophical and the practical—not only for ourselves, but also for our colleagues,

Working with Faculty to Design Undergraduate Information Literacy Programs: A How-To-Do-It Manual for Librarians is the result of our efforts. Here is the model that we used to design information literacy programs that tie into a curriculum and are implemented with faculty awareness and commitment. We call it a "model" because it is predicated on four basic considerations we found to be crucial in developing and implementing successful information literacy instruction programs:

—establishing partnerships with the teaching faculty in designing a curriculum-integrated instructional program;
—creating content and class assignments for a course unit, a stand-alone session, or a credit course;
—evaluating student comprehension and application of information literacy competencies and instructional methodologies used;
—managing administrative tasks such as drafting policy statements, scheduling, designing electronic classrooms, and organizing instructional materials.

We wrote *Working with Faculty to Design Undergraduate Information Literacy Programs* primarily for librarians in undergraduate academic libraries, but it is also useful for faculty members who are committed to helping students develop their information-seeking skills. Librarians or teachers working with advanced placement high school students will also appreciate *Working with Faculty* for the useful ideas, programs, and methods of integrating information literacy instruction with the curriculum.

Working with Faculty to Design Undergraduate Information Literacy Programs is intended to provide readers with the tools to plan, develop, create, implement, administer, and evaluate information literacy programs. With this goal in mind, we begin by defining information literacy and conclude with the administrative issues of managing an instructional program. Along the way, we include outlines for course-integrated and stand-alone presentations, a syllabus for a credit course on accessing and evaluating information, sample assignments and exercises, sample survey and evaluation instruments, a sample policy statement for instructional services, and practical tips on incorporating instructional technologies into class presentations and assignments.

Chapter 1 lays the foundation by defining information literacy, explaining its importance in today's society, and examining the implications of the faculty culture in designing curriculum-integrated instruction.

Strategies and practical methods to assess faculty attitudes towards incorporating information literacy instruction into class presentations and assignments are covered in Chapter 2, as well as suggestions for improving faculty information literacy.

Chapters 3 through 5 provide detailed advice on creating the content and assignments for a course-integrated unit, a stand-alone presentation, and a credit course respectively.

The need for conducting periodic assessments, the reasons for using a variety of measures to evaluate how students are progressing, the effectiveness of the instructional methodologies in teaching students information literacy competencies, and examples of evaluation instruments are examined in Chapter 6. This chapter also includes a number of evaluation instruments. Chapter 7 covers the use and development of video programs, presentation software programs, and Web tutorials for presentations and assignments.

Chapter 8 provides practical information on managing an instructional program (e.g., scheduling, organizing materials, designing electronic classrooms, annual reports, and keeping current with new developments in teaching methodologies and issues).

The Information Age is putting more demands on teachers and students. Using *Working with Faculty to Design Undergraduate Information Literacy Programs* will help enhance your skills and form more productive relationships with students and faculty.

ACKNOWLEDGMENTS

We would like to thank our colleagues for their support and contributions. Special thanks go to Debra Oswald for her editing assistance and for permitting us to use various forms and policies that she developed. John Burke was especially helpful with his expertise in instructional technologies. The overview of multimedia production was created by H. Michael Sanders. Steve Botos designed a number of figures that appear in this book.

We also acknowledge the continuing support provided by the staff members of the University of Cincinnati College of Applied Science Library and the Raymond Walters College Library: Nancy Hunter, Susan Hight, and Margie Kroeger.

1 LAYING THE FOUNDATION

In writing this book, we consciously chose to use the phrase "information literacy" rather than "bibliographic instruction." Some may question whether there is a significant difference between these two terms, and they may believe they are one and the same. But in our opinion these two terms are distinct. First, bibliographic instruction encompasses a variety of methods and techniques to teach students the skills to locate and evaluate information resources. Information literacy is the outcome that students achieve in being able to apply these skills throughout educational, professional, and personal lives. Second, bibliographic instruction focuses upon the librarian's development and use of instructional methods; information literacy emphasizes the student's acquisition and effective application of the skills learned through bibliographic instruction. Third, the term "bibliographic" implies the traditional concept of print, but "information" is inclusive, encompassing all types of formats—print, media, and electronic.

By making these distinctions, we are not implying, however, that information literacy is superior to bibliographic instruction. You cannot achieve the goal of developing information-literate students without using bibliographic instruction methods. Furthermore, the ultimate objective of teaching students information research skills is to produce independent learners. We elected to use "information literacy" to emphasize the outcome of the instructional process—students who cannot only locate and retrieve information, but also evaluate and apply the use of this information appropriately. To accomplish this goal, it is necessary to create partnerships with the faculty in our academic institutions to design and implement successful programs.

This chapter defines information literacy and describes its importance to our society. It also examines the faculty culture and why librarians often have difficulty in gaining the cooperation and support needed to incorporate information literacy instruction into the curriculum.

DEFINING INFORMATION LITERACY

Succinctly stated, information literacy is the ability to access, evaluate, and apply information effectively to situations requiring decision making, problem solving, or the acquisition of knowledge. Such a brief definition, however, belies the complexity of this concept and all that it implies. To become information literate, one must progress from the acquisition of facts about specific resources and mechanical procedures, to the ability to locate data, to the evaluation of the accuracy and quality of this information, to the final application of this information to a given circumstance. Moreover, the questions of how individuals acquire these abilities, who is responsible for teaching these concepts, and why it is necessary for individuals to be information literate are interwoven into the understanding of what information literacy is.

Shirley J. Behrens has examined information literacy's evolution from the 1970s to the 1990s and identified significant trends regarding the librarian's role in the information literacy movement.[1] Of the many notable publications that Behrens analyzes, there are three that are of particular importance. In 1974, Paul Zurkowski, president of the Information Industry Association, was the first person to define information literacy in a proposal submitted to the National Commission on Libraries and Information Science: "People trained in the application of information resources to their work can be called information literates. They have learned techniques and skills for utilizing the wide range of information tools as well as primary sources in molding information solutions to their problems."[2] Behrens identifies three key elements in Zurkowski's definition: (1) the utilization of information resources in the work environment; (2) the need for skills to use these information resources; and (3) the use of information in problem solving.[3]

The second notable publication is *Information Literacy: Revolution in the Library*, by Patricia S. Breivik and E. Gordon Gee. When published, Breivik was the library director and Gee was the president at the University of Colorado in Denver. One of the principle themes put forth by Breivik and Gee is the essential role libraries and librarians have in the education process, especially in instructing students to acquire lifelong learning abilities: "Libraries are where the knowledge of all disciplines is related within a meaningful framework. Libraries provide a model for the information environment in which graduates will need to work and live. Libraries are a natural environment for problem-solving within the unlimited universe of information. Libraries provide the framework for synthesizing specialized knowledge into broader societal contexts. And finally, libraries and librarians can help students master critical information-literacy skills."[4] To achieve this educational goal, Breivik and Gee state that partnerships must be forged among the library, university administration, faculty, and the business community.[5] As a case in point, the University of Colorado successfully implemented information literacy instruction across the curriculum through such partnerships.

The third significant publication is the 1989 report prepared by the American Library Association Presidential Committee on Information Literacy. In this report, ALA gives this definition of information literacy: "To be information literate, a person must be able to recognize when information is needed and have the ability to locate, evaluate, and use effectively the needed information. . . . They are people prepared for lifelong learning, because they can always find the information needed for any task or decision at hand."[6] What is of particular importance concerning this report is the identification of specific skills needed to access, evaluate, and apply information. These skills include: knowing when there is a need for information; identifying the information needed to address the situation at hand; locating the necessary information; evaluating the information; organizing the information; and applying the information appropriately to resolve a problem or make a decision.[7] The report further states that a new learning model, called resource-based learning, must be introduced to teach individuals to become information literate. Rather than relying primarily upon textbooks and lectures, students must be able to locate and use a variety of information resources that will be available throughout their lives. Finally, the ALA report emphasizes the importance of information literacy for individuals to address personal information needs, to function in the workplace, and to participate in society as knowledgeable citizens.[8]

Behrens identifies thirteen elements that have been incorporated into our current understanding of information literacy. Key elements include:

- specific attitudes, including the recognition of a need for information, a willingness to locate and apply information, and an appreciation of the value of information
- more complex critical thinking skills, such as comprehension and evaluation
- a definition that encompasses much more than library or computer skills
- the need for a major shift in bibliographic instruction programs to encompass the wide range of skills necessary for information literacy
- the development of partnerships between librarians and faculty to make possible the effective teaching of information literacy.[9]

Behrens also examines the literature in the early 1990s and identifies three major trends: the continual development and implementation of models and theories for information literacy curricula; the recognition that information literacy is a part of a continuum incorporating both the traditional skills of reading and writing, as well as highly developed critical-thinking abilities; and the evaluation by librarians of their role in participating in the teaching of information literacy.[10]

The definition of information literacy continues to evolve. Gretchen McCord Hoffman has challenged the notion of information literacy as a process to a final outcome of specific skills. Instead, she states that " . . . we should regard it [information literacy] as a lifelong process in which library instruction is only one step. We need to think of ourselves as a part of the process of information literacy, as facilitators, rather than as deliverers of a goal."[11]

In this brief review of the published literature from the 1970s to the present, it is evident that the concept of information literacy has evolved from the emphasis upon its application in the workplace to the recognition of its importance for individuals to become lifelong learners and informed citizens. In this environment, it is essential that librarians create partnerships with the faculty to implement a successful information literacy curriculum.

THE IMPORTANCE OF INFORMATION LITERACY

As librarians, we certainly understand why information literacy is essential; however, we face a number of challenges in sharing that understanding. First, we must change the misconception believed by students (and sometimes faculty) that knowing how to use a computer is the same as knowing how to find information. Computer literacy is only one of the many skills needed to access and retrieve information. Second, we must stress the importance of evaluating the retrieved information, and not just the process of knowing how to use indexes, online catalogs, or CD-ROM databases. The ability to evaluate information resources has always been necessary, but it is now more critical than ever. In addition to the thousands of books, journals, and newspapers published each year and the innumerable television and radio station broadcasts, there are well over a million (and counting) Internet sites. Anyone can create a Web site and publish all sorts of information. The difficulty for the Internet searcher is to discern the credentials of these Web authors and the accuracy of the information included on their sites. Third, we must find ways of encouraging students to recognize not only that they need to find information but also that the information they retrieve has intrinsic value. The ALA Presidential Committee on Information Literacy report states: "Information literacy is a survival skill in the information age. Instead of drowning in the abundance of information that floods their lives, information-literate people know how to find, evaluate, and use information effectively . . . whether the information they select comes from a computer, a book, a government agency, a film or any number of other possible resources."[12]

As discussed earlier in this chapter, one of the original definitions of information literacy included the application of information to make decisions in the workplace. In reviewing the business literature, it is evident that chief executive officers, managers, and human resources personnel understand the need for an information literate work force. The very nature of work is changing radically as the United States continues to evolve from a manufacturing to an information-based economy. Consequently, there is a growing need for highly skilled and well-educated workers who are able to analyze and apply information—in other words, the knowledge worker. Examples of occupations that require large numbers of knowledge workers include health care, computer software development, education, government administration, and finance. Peter Drucker defines the characteristics of knowledge workers as requiring "a good deal of formal education and the ability to acquire and apply theoretical and analytical knowledge . . . Above all, they require a habit of continuous learning."[13] A recent estimate for the number of knowledge workers in the United States work force is 39 percent and growing.[14] Unless more people enter the work force with information literacy skills, it is possible that 20 percent of available jobs will go unfilled by the year 2000.[15]

Related to the need for an information literate work force is the perception of many CEOs of the poor quality of public education. In a 1990 Fortune 500 survey, 76 percent of the CEO respondents indicated that public education worsens rather than improves the quality of the U.S. work force.[16] Another survey reveals that most Fortune 500 executives believe that graduates from public education institutions entering the work force are unable to read and write, let alone think critically, analyze data, and resolve problems.[17] Although based on perception, the results of these surveys emphasize the need to include information literacy as a core competency, along with reading and writing. Therefore, the development of information literacy skills is essential both to the individual for gainful employment and to businesses to thrive and compete successfully in the global market.

In a democratic society, citizens have the right to make choices and decisions that impact their lives, communities, and their government. Thus, the ability to access, evaluate, and apply information is crucial to the democratic process. In 1976, U.S. Representative Major R. Owens stated: "Information literacy is needed to guarantee the survival of democratic institutions. All men are created equal, but voters with information resources are in a position to make more intelligent decisions than citizens who are information illiterates. The application of information resources to the process of decision making to fulfill civic responsibilities is a vital necessity."[18]

FACULTY CULTURE AND IMPLICATIONS FOR INFORMATION LITERACY INSTRUCTION

Although many librarians view themselves as teachers and may have faculty status and rank, some faculty may not perceive librarians as colleagues engaged in the education process. Some faculty may regard the library's collections as essential but disregard the need for their students to learn how to use these collections. Thus, librarians continually struggle to gain a foothold in the curriculum to instruct students on the important research skills and resources they will need, both for the short and long term. Unfortunately, the usual scenario is a single fifty-minute presentation during which the librarian must cover everything from basic research skills to complex search strategies in specialized databases. Librarians have redefined their roles as teachers, especially in the past twenty years, but some faculty may continue to resist the integration of information literacy instruction into their curricula.

Why is this, and why do librarians sometimes have a difficult time in gaining wider acceptance by the faculty? Some of the answers may be found in Larry Hardesty's article, "Faculty Culture and Bibliographic Instruction: An Exploratory Analysis," which provides an excellent review of the characteristics of the faculty culture and the subsequent attitudes faculty often have toward librarians. The primary responsibility of the faculty is to pursue and disseminate knowledge through teaching, research, and publication. What has emerged in current American higher education is the emphasis upon research and publication, often at the expense of teaching. Furthermore, those faculty who are engaged in scholarly research often do not value other faculty involved in professional practice. That being the case, librarians may not be highly regarded within the academic community.[19] Ironically, college faculty are not taught how to teach and often view teaching as an art, rather than as a discipline with its own knowledge base. Because faculty are valued for what they know, teaching is often perceived as just a method of communicating to students knowledge of their discipline.[20]

Another important aspect of the faculty culture is its strong belief in academic freedom and professional autonomy. It is the right, as well as the responsibility, of the faculty member to decide the course content and assignments, educational objectives, and methods of instruction. Hardesty states that this belief system "militates against inviting others, such as librarians to share in the teaching process."[21]

Although academic institutions are often characterized as hotbeds of radical thought, in reality they are conservative in action. Faculty resist change because they lack the time to make any changes. The "publish or perish syndrome," the increased competition for shrinking research funding, and the incredible number of committee meetings—all of these factors reduce the time that a faculty member could be working upon curriculum development and revision. Moreover, faculty governance is based upon consensus, which slows down the decision-making process and the ability to implement changes in a timely manner.[22]

In summary, Hardesty states:

> The focus here, then, is on significant aspects of the development of modern faculty culture in the United States with its emphasis on research and content and de-emphasis on teaching and process. The result is a highly autonomous, often isolated, faculty faced with considerable pressures, including the lack of time, to perform in areas in which its members are not particularly well-trained (teaching) or well-supported either by their institutions or the other members of the profession. The result is a culture characterized by a resistance to change, particularly a change promoted by those (such as librarians) who are not perceived as sharing fully in the culture and are not promoting values (bibliographic instruction) compatible with it.[23]

All is not bleak, however—otherwise, we would not have given up a year's worth of "free" time to write this book! A review of the literature on information literacy and bibliographic instruction, turns up many cases of successful programs in a variety of academic settings. The students that librarians taught yesterday are today's (and tomorrow's) faculty. Hardesty includes several studies that indicate a correlation between faculty members' opinions of information literacy instruction and how they learned library-research skills as undergraduates: faculty who learned from librarians are more likely to include information literacy instruction for their students.[24] Hardesty concludes his article: "Idealism has long been a trait of bibliographic instruction librarians and, combined with a better understanding of, and sensitivity to, faculty culture, bibliographic instruction may become part of the culture as it has become a part of the culture of librarians."[25] It is with this idealism, tempered with experience and research, that we write this book.

NOTES

1. Shirley J. Behrens, "A Conceptual Analysis and Historical Overview of Information Literacy," *College & Research Libraries* 55 (July 1994): 309.
2. Paul G. Zurkowski, *The Information Service Environment Relationship and Priorities* (Washington, D.C.: National Commission on Libraries and Information Service, 1974), p. 6.
3. Behrens, "A Conceptual Analysis," p. 310.
4. Patricia S. Breivik and E. Gordon Gee, *Information Literacy: Revolution in the Library* (New York: Macmillan, 1989), p. 28.
5. *Ibid.*, pp. 85–106, 31–52, 69–83.
6. American Library Association Presidential Committee on Information Literacy, *Final Report* (Chicago: American Library Association, 1989), p. 1.
7. Behrens, "A Conceptual Analysis," p. 316.
8. ALA Presidential Committee on Information Literacy, *Final Report*, p. 7.
9. Behrens, "A Conceptual Analysis," pp. 316–317.
10. *Ibid.*, pp. 317–319.
11. Gretchen McCord Hoffman, "Library Instruction in Transition: Questioning Current Views," in *Finding Common Ground: Creating the Library of the Future Without Diminishing the Library of the Past,* ed. Cheryl M. LaGuardia and Barbara A. Mitchell (New York: Neal-Schuman, 1997).
12. ALA Presidential Committee on Information Literacy, *Final Report*, p. 6.
13. Peter F. Drucker, *Managing in a Time of Great Change* (New York: Truman Talley Books/Dutton, 1995), p. 226.
14. James Aley, "Where the Jobs Are," *Fortune* 132 (September 18, 1995): 53.
15. "Knowledge Workers in Demand through Year 2000," *Managing Office Technology* 42 (January 1997): 22.
16. Andrew Erdman, "How to Make Workers Better," *Fortune* 122 (October 22, 1990): 75.
17. John Nidds and James McGerald, "Corporations View Public Education," *Principle* 74 (March 1995): 22–23.
18. Major Owens, "State Government and Libraries," *Library Journal* 101 (January 1, 1976): 27.
19. Larry Hardesty, "Faculty Culture and Bibliographic Instruction: An Exploratory Analysis," *Library Trends* 44 (Fall 1995): 348–349.
20. *Ibid.*, p. 350.
21. *Ibid.*, p. 352.

22. *Ibid.*, pp. 352–353.
23. *Ibid.*, p. 354.
24. *Ibid.*, p. 360.
25. *Ibid.*, p. 363.

2 FACULTY AND INFORMATION LITERACY

A prominent theme in library literature is the need for librarian-faculty cooperation for successful information literacy efforts. Librarians are well aware of the critical role that faculty play in developing courses and assignments that require students to find and use information from a variety of sources:

- The faculty are the chief motivators of student use of the library through the cursory use of reserve materials or in-depth research assignments.
- The faculty provide class time for the librarian to present course-integrated, research skills sessions.
- The faculty directly influence the attitudes that students form about the library and its usefulness in their courses and their future careers.[1]

Librarians have put Herculean efforts into creating information literacy programs for students. Unfortunately, many programs have been developed without the input of faculty.[2] Or, if faculty have been involved, it was only to discuss a brief overview of what is to be covered in the library session. The development of a meaningful assignment with input from both librarian and faculty is overlooked. In truth, faculty ambivalence toward the need for student information literacy training impedes progress toward an acceptable model for teaching library skills.[3]

In addition, the emphasis in these programs is on educating students and neglects the information literacy education of faculty.[4] Librarians themselves are overwhelmed by the plethora of new products and services being introduced at an ever-increasing rate in libraries, so imagine the difficulties that faculty face. Faculty require more support than ever in keeping up with new information sources in their subject specialties.

Given the importance of faculty to any information literacy effort, it is necessary to understand faculty attitudes toward the library. And it is necessary that faculty themselves be information literate.

ASSESSING YOUR FACULTY'S ATTITUDES AND NEEDS

Before undertaking any major change in your information literacy program, it is advisable to have an understanding of your faculty's needs and attitudes. There are numerous methods for obtaining feedback from your faculty, but, judging from the literature, surveys are the most popular means. Other choices include individual faculty interviews and focus groups. A thorough information-gathering effort may involve all these.

Before choosing your method of assessing faculty attitudes, and before you compose the first question, determine the purpose of the exercise. Are you assessing faculty attitudes toward the library, the librarians, the librarians as teaching partners, or an existing bibliographic-instruction program? Are you trying to determine the faculty's current level of participation in your information literacy program, or their willingness to participate in a new program? Do you want to assess your faculty's information needs, or their information-seeking habits? Do you want to assess your students' information needs as perceived by the faculty? Once you have determined what information you are seeking, determine which method of assessment suits your situation.

SURVEYS

Faculty surveys are valuable tools for successfully gathering information from a large number of faculty representing many departments. They are less labor intensive than focus groups or individual interviews. If it is important in your situation to get opinions from the largest number of faculty possible, and if the personnel that you can devote to the project is limited, then a survey may be the appropriate tool.

Fifteen Tips for Creating a Survey

The following general tips will help you to create a survey that will gather useful information.

1. Select your target audience. Are you surveying faculty from one department or the entire institution? Do you wish to include adjunct faculty or only full-time faculty? If your target audience is too large, you may want to choose a representative group to survey. Creating a random sample that is truly representative of your total constituency can do this. (Software packages are available for using this method.)

2. Determine the purpose of the survey and carefully focus your survey questions to provide that information.
3. Construct your survey questions in a neutral, unbiased manner that will not influence the answers.
4. Do not make the survey too lengthy. The longer the survey, the less likely faculty will take the time to answer it.
5. Convey the purpose of the survey to your faculty. Most will want to know how you will use the information you are gathering before they spend their valuable time answering your questions.
6. Offer to publish the results of the survey in a publication that the faculty receive such as a library newsletter. If that is not an option, offer to send a letter with the results to any faculty members indicating interest. Faculty may be more likely to participate if they have an opportunity to see the results of the survey.
7. Demographic information on the responding faculty can be valuable in interpreting the responses.
8. Questions can be either open ended or closed ended. In open-ended questions, the respondent provides an answer. In closed-ended questions, the respondent selects a predetermined answer. Open-ended questions can provide more detailed information, but can be more difficult to tabulate. Closed-ended questions are easier to tabulate but are limited in the information they can provide. Try to use a combination in your survey.
9. Using rankings to determine interest level in various services can be useful in times of limited library staff. The librarians at Gallaudet University have created surveys that effectively use questions with rankings.[5]
10. Test your survey by having nonlibrary personnel (preferably several faculty members) answer the survey to be sure that the questions are clear and that any library terminology is well defined.
11. Time the distribution of the survey to an appropriate period of the academic calendar when faculty will have the opportunity to complete it. Sending surveys during break week could negatively affect your return rate.
12. Allow approximately ten to fourteen days for responses. If you give a longer period of time, surveys will be set aside and then forgotten.
13. A follow-up mailing approximately one week after the first mailing may increase the likelihood of responses. This can be a letter or post card reminding respondents of the importance of the survey and asking that they return it by the appropriate due date.

14. Speak directly to department heads or library advisory committee members to let them know the importance of the survey and ask them to mention it at departmental meetings.
15. Send a thank-you note to all respondents. Or, if the survey is anonymous, send cards to everyone who received the original survey thanking them for their response and encouraging them to respond if they did not do so.

There are many excellent examples of faculty-assessment surveys in the literature (see the end of this chapter for suggested for further reading on the topic). Figure 2.1 provides a sample library-services survey that was distributed to faculty members of the Department of Psychology of the University of Cincinnati. This in-depth survey was created by Randall Roberts of the Training and Educational Services Department. Mr. Roberts was seeking faculty feedback on the library's training opportunities as well as the collections and other services.

Figure 2.1   Library Services Survey: Faculty

Unless otherwise instructed, please record your response by circling the appropriate number on the scale following each question or statement. If you have no opinion on a survey question or statement, please circle "No Opinion."

1. How often do you access library resources (includes either actual visits to the library or online access to library resources)?
    Number of times per week:

Less than 1	*2–5*	*6–9*	*10–14*	*More than 14*	*No Opinion*

2. Library-related research (access to books, journals, indexes, information databases, etc., provided by the library) important for the support of instruction and research in your field.

Strongly Disagree	*1*	*2*	*3*	*4*	*5*	*Strongly Agree*	*No Opinion*

3. Libraries fulfill your instructional and research needs.

Strongly Disagree	*1*	*2*	*3*	*4*	*5*	*Strongly Agree*	*No Opinion*

4. How often do you give assignments that require your students to use the library's resources?
    Number of times per course:

0	*1–2*	*3–4*	*5–6*	*More than 6*

5. Your experience with the following library services has been satisfactory. [Please record your answer in the column labeled, "Degree of Agreement."]

Strongly Disagree	*1*	*2*	*3*	*4*	*5*	*Strongly Agree*	*No Opinion – 6*

Library Services	**Degree of Agreement**
Patron initiated borrowing (Patron initiates borrowing procedure electronically via OhioLINK)	
Traditional Interlibrary Loan Service for retrieval of books or journal articles not held by U.C.	
Library Information Desk	
Library Reference Consultation Office	
Library Reserves Department	
Library Multimedia Services Department	

6. Your undergraduate students can effectively use the library and its resources.

Strongly Disagree	1	2	3	4	5	Strongly Agree	No Opinion

7. Your graduate students can effectively use the library and its resources.

Strongly Disagree	1	2	3	4	5	Strongly Agree	No Opinion

8. Basic instruction in the use of the library and its resources is a vital component of the undergraduate student's education.

Strongly Disagree	1	2	3	4	5	Strongly Agree	No Opinion

9. Advanced instruction on the use of specialized library resources in your field is a vital component of the graduate student's education.

Strongly Disagree	1	2	3	4	5	Strongly Agree	No Opinion

10. You are generally satisfied with your level of competence with the library's electronic research tools in your field.

Strongly Disagree	1	2	3	4	5	Strongly Agree	No Opinion

11. The following library instruction options are effective methods for the delivery of library-related instruction for both students and faculty. Indicate your degree of agreement in both columns.

	Strongly Disagree	1	2	3	4	5	Strongly Agree	No Opinion

Instruction options	Students	Faculty
General library-instruction session for a single class		N/A
Subject or specific resource instructional session for a single class		N/A
Course-integrated library instruction class*		N/A
Computer-based instruction for general library resources (independent-learning tool)		
Computer-based instruction for specific research materials (independent-learning tool)		
Workshops (hands on) for specific library-related resources, e.g. Internet		
Series of classes or workshops focused on resources in one discipline		
One-credit-hour course on information literacy with focus on resources in your field		N/A
Two-credit-hour course on information literacy with focus on resources in your field		N/A
Three-credit-hour course on information literacy with focus on resources in your field		N/A
Library orientation tours		
YOUR SUGGESTIONS:	N/A	N/A

_____

_____

_____

*Collaborative effort between the course instructor and a librarian to achieve a specific outcome, for example, research paper.

12. The following library workshops would be useful to you or your students. Please indicate your degree of agreement in both columns.

	Strongly Disagree	1	2	3	4	5	Strongly Agree	No Opinion – 6

Name of workshop with short description	Students	Faculty
Introductory workshop on how to use the primary research database for literature in your field		
Uncover/REVEAL (Introductory workshop on a database of 17,000+ journals and books; includes instruction on REVEAL, a free current-awareness service)		
World Wide Web (General workshop about the Web)		
Web search engines (Workshop about selected Web search engines)		
Resources on the Web (Workshop on selected resources in your field)		
UCLID/OhioLINK (Workshop on searching our local and statewide online catalog)		
Downloading from UCLID (Specialized workshop about downloading records from UCLID, OhioLINK, and any of the "UCLID-like" electronic databases.)		
ProCite (Specialized workshop on the development and maintenance of your own electronic database of citations downloaded from UCLID and other databases; instruction includes the creation of bibliographies [reference lists] under various style manuals)		
Test resources (Workshop on finding information about tests)		
Resources (General workshop on reference tools in your field)		
Full-text databases (General workshop on use of electronic full-text resources)		
PowerPoint (Introductory workshop on use of this graphical computer-presentation software)		
Windows 95 (Introductory workshop on the navigation features and files management in Windows 95)		

YOUR SUGGESTIONS:

_____

_____

13. With respect to your teaching responsibilities, the library's book collection is adequate.

| | Strongly Disagree | 1 | 2 | 3 | 4 | 5 | Strongly Agree | No Opinion |

14. With respect to your research requirements, the library's book collection is adequate.

| | Strongly Disagree | 1 | 2 | 3 | 4 | 5 | Strongly Agree | No Opinion |

15. With respect to your teaching responsibilities, the library's periodical collection is adequate.

| | Strongly Disagree | 1 | 2 | 3 | 4 | 5 | Strongly Agree | No Opinion |

16. With respect to your research requirements, the library's periodical collection is adequate.

| | Strongly Disagree | 1 | 2 | 3 | 4 | 5 | Strongly Agree | No Opinion |

17. Your department should have a standing library committee that meets regularly with a library liaison to discuss library materials needs, library service requirements, curricula changes, etc.

| | Strongly Disagree | 1 | 2 | 3 | 4 | 5 | Strongly Agree | No Opinion |

18. Please indicate your interest in a computerized current-awareness service that would provide you with a regular update of published research (books and articles) in your area.

| | Strongly Disagree | 1 | 2 | 3 | 4 | 5 | Strongly Agree | No Opinion |

Your additional comments or suggestions on library services are welcome.

_____

_____

_____

Please indicate your area(s) of specialization in your field: _____

Your name (optional): _____

Thank you for your time and interest. Please return this survey by inserting it in the enclosed, preaddressed envelope.

INDIVIDUAL INTERVIEWS

Your survey can also be administered in person instead of by the respondent. This would involve a library staff member making an appointment to interview a faculty member either in the office or by telephone. When a library staff member makes an appointment with a faculty member to get ideas on library programs, you are guaranteed to get answers. In this scenario, open-ended questions work best, giving the faculty member every opportunity to be creative with suggestions and ideas for improvements. The downside of individual interviews is that it is very labor intensive. This approach can generally only be used for small numbers of faculty.

FOCUS GROUPS

Focus groups are defined as a "qualitative research technique used to obtain data about feelings and opinions of small groups of participants about a given problem, experience, or service."[6] Focus groups, used by marketing research firms since the 1950s and have been successfully used by libraries to elicit the attitudes of their constituency. Focus groups can be an excellent source of suggestions for improvements in library services. Although they take a lot of time to organize and run, focus groups have the advantage over surveys of allowing for interaction between participants and moderators.

Twelve Tips for Running a Focus Group

The following general tips will help you plan your focus group.

1. The most important rule to remember when considering a focus group is to use trained focus-group moderators. Their training instills the skills that allows them to guide the discussion, keep it on the subject, but not control the discussion. The quality of your focus-group moderator will make or break your session.
2. Use a focus-group moderator who is not a member of the library staff. Focus-group moderators must be flexible and have some distance from the outcome of the discussion. If a focus group produces negative feedback, it is not useful for the moderator to become defensive or to try to give reasons for the "way things are."
3. Librarians should not observe the focus-group sessions. This could inhibit the discussions.
4. Try to hold your focus group in a conference room in a building closest to the faculty involved in the group; you may get better participation.
5. Establish specific objectives before conducting the sessions. It

is recommended that a focus-group session should be centered on a single theme.

6. Work with your focus-group moderator to develop the list of questions for the focus group and to answer any questions the moderator has on library jargon or procedures.
7. The number of focus-group participants is usually limited to between seven and ten.
8. Give the participants a detailed list of questions you would like their feedback on. This can help keep the discussion moving.
9. Try to have present a scribe who is not a focus-group participant to write down what is said. Ideas can come fast and furiously, and it is difficult for the moderator both to guide the discussion and to take notes. Taping the session is not recommended, as participants may feel inhibited by this.
10. The scribe and the moderator should write a thorough report as soon after the session as possible.
11. The right number of focus-group sessions to have depends on how many faculty are in your institution and if you feel you require a cross-section of this group. It also depends on the complexity of the issues you want addressed and the consistency of findings from session to session. An experienced focus-group moderator should be able to help you determine the right number of sessions.
12. Provide feedback to the participants on the results of the focus group. If any changes are made as a result of suggestions brought forward in the session, faculty will feel that their time has been well spent.

EDUCATING FACULTY FIRST

Given the importance of the faculty in the information literacy process, librarians need to focus their teaching efforts on their faculty first. Unless faculty are information literate themselves, students will not be. As you undertake a program of faculty education, you will find the same varying levels of ability in using complex library resources in faculty as you find in students.

TEN OPPORTUNITIES TO EDUCATE FACULTY

Librarians must become involved and highly visible campuswide. Since every academic institution is unique, different opportunities will present themselves at different institutions. Be poised to take advantage of any opportunity that presents itself—or create your own opportunities. Following are ten ideas to get you started.

1. Meet New Faculty.

New faculty workshops and orientations are golden opportunities to meet new faculty and present an overview of the library's collection and services. But don't stop there! Arrange meet the new faculty member in his or her office to demonstrate access to electronic resources from the desktop. A one-on-one meeting will help you to establish the faculty member's level of information literacy and will give you an opportunity to offer further assistance. When faculty members feel comfortable with their knowledge of the library, they are more likely to require their students to use its resources.

2. Explain Library Services at Departmental Meetings.

Most faculty are pressed for time and may find it difficult to attend extra workshops on library resources. However, most faculty already have attendance at their departmental meeting on their calendar. Work with the department head to arrange a library-resources presentation at a regular meeting. This gives you a great opportunity to talk to a large number of department faculty members and to focus your presentation on those specialized resources that everyone in the department will find interesting, instead of trying to cover a broad array of resources. Encourage department members to make appointments for one-on-one orientations to specific resources.

3. Offer Faculty-Only Workshops in the Use of Research Resources.

Faculty may be hesitant to attend open research-skills sessions that the library offers. Some faculty may be embarrassed that they do not know everything there is to know about the library. Some faculty may not want to have their students observe them as they struggle to learn a new resource. If time and staffing permit, it may be valuable to offer a faculty-only workshop series. Try to have numerous library staff members present at these workshops to provide one-on-one instruction. Everyone, including faculty, appreciates personal attention.

4. Take Advantage of Faculty Retreats.

Plan presentations for faculty retreats on innovative teaching methods that incorporate information literacy concepts across the curriculum or on new information products or services in the library. If a presentation is not possible, serve on the organizing committee for the faculty retreat. The assistance will be appreciated, and librarians will become more visible and accepted as colleagues through these efforts.

5. Join the Faculty Brown-Bag-Lunch Series.

Many campuses have this type of lecture series, or something similar. If your campus does not have a brown-bag-lecture series already established, start one at the library. It gives librarians a perfect opportunity to meet with a small group of faculty from a cross-section of their campus.

If you have an opportunity to lecture, choose your topic wisely. Offer an eye-catching title and description to draw a good turnout. This sort of presentation is useful both for educating faculty on the latest library resources and demonstrating to faculty the teaching quality of librarians. An example of a topic that might draw faculty would be "Research Skills Across the Curriculum: Integrating Information Literacy Skills into Your Classroom." If your brown-bag lunch is for faculty members of one department, focus your presentation on specific new resources of interest to those department members, such as the latest "table of contents" service or full-text document delivery service for specialized journals in their field. Avoid topics that imply that an instructor needs to be refreshed in how or what to teach.

6. Be Active in the "Center for Teaching Excellence."

Most colleges and universities create this type of center to offer support to their teaching faculty. Some institutions also focus these efforts on their graduate or teaching assistants. This is the perfect starting point for introducing information literacy skills to graduate and teaching assistants who are future faculty.

7. Develop a Research Component for "Writing Across the Curriculum" Workshops.

It can be valuable to develop a research-skills component that dovetails with any "writing across the curriculum" workshops that your institution sponsors. Faculty attend these workshops to learn to incorporate new skills into their teaching repertoire. They should be open to ideas on incorporating research skills into their classes.

8. Write Articles in Professional Journals Other than Library Journals.

Articles written about the importance of information literacy skills appear mainly in library literature. Jacobson and Vallely did an exhaustive search and analysis of nonlibrary journals, which pointed up the appalling lack of articles on information literacy.[7] We are not getting our message to the appropriate audience. Consider how useful and effective articles on the importance of information literacy would be if they were read by teaching faculty. One of the best examples that comes to mind of an information literacy article in a nonlibrary journal was an article in the March 20, 1998 issue of *The Chronicle of Higher Education*.[8] The article, which emphasizes the roles of both faculty and librarians in teaching students to be critical readers, thinkers, and writers, reached far more teaching faculty than one in *Library Journal* could ever hope to.

If you have a successful experience in team teaching information literacy skills, approach the faculty member with the idea of collaborating on an article about the experience for publication in a nonlibrary journal. This could provide a number of benefits. Not only will you be meeting publishing requirements, but also the article will reach the teaching faculty. Examples of nonlibrary journals to publish in are far too numerous to list, but education-oriented journals such as *The Chronicle of Higher Education* and *Change* are good choices, as are more specialized journals such as the *Journal of Chemical Education* or *ASEE Prism* (American Society for Engineering Education's publication).

9. Attend Cultural and Social Events with Faculty.

This approach could enhance the collegial spirit within an institution. For librarians who work best in informal settings, this approach can be successful in both making friends and promoting the library and its resources.

10. Offer a Summer Institute.

Most of the suggestions listed above represent one-shot presentations for faculty members. Librarians are already aware that one-shot teaching opportunities with students may have less-than-satisfactory results. Why would we anticipate that these would be any more successful with faculty?

If librarians have both the financial and the personnel resources to offer competitive summer institute grants for information literacy training for their faculty, they will see better results. Faculty may require the enticement of money and the stature of receiving a grant before they are willing to participate.

A typical curriculum for an information literacy summer institute could be:

- how to use the library's latest information technologies
- how to integrate these information technologies into the classroom
- how to create meaningful, effective research assignments for students.

Successful completion of the information literacy summer institute would require that a faculty member either create a new course syllabus or revise an existing course syllabus and include class assignments that integrate information literacy skills into the course subject matter.

OBTAINING FACULTY COOPERATION FOR AN UNDERGRADUATE INFORMATION LITERACY PROGRAM

Once your faculty is up to speed, your next step is to obtain faculty support for an undergraduate information literacy program. Unfortunately, you may not end up with the undergraduate information literacy program envisioned. An effective incorporation of information literacy skills requires extensive revision of course plans by the faculty—something that does not happen easily. It requires intense teamwork between librarians and faculty and resource commitment from the library and the institution's leaders. It was noted by Gibson that "the real challenge of the 1990s is for instructional librarians to develop the necessary political skills to convince faculty colleagues and administrators that there is a coherent set of intellectual skills in information seeking that can be taught, evaluated and dovetailed with the larger goals of the institution."[9]

INFORMATION LITERACY COMPETENCIES

To incorporate information literacy skills effectively into the curriculum, librarians should work closely with faculty to identify core information literacy competencies that students should possess. Examples of information literacy competency statements can be found in the print literature and on the Web. Most are based on the American Library Association's definition of information literacy.

For example, a proposal for establishing information literacy competencies was put forward by the University of Cincinnati Access College librarians through the Access Colleges Freshman English Committee (see Figure 2.2). This Committee is comprised of all Freshman English instructors of the four Access Colleges of the University of Cincinnati. The proposal was accepted.

Figure 2.2 Proposal to Incorporate Information Literacy Competencies into Freshman English Curriculum

With the explosion of information resources in a variety of formats (e.g., paper, Web, intranet databases, other multimedia resources), it is essential that students be information literate. Information literacy is defined as the ability to locate, evaluate, and effectively use needed information. Attached to this proposal is a brochure prepared by the American Library Association that describes the importance of acquiring and maintaining information skills for current and lifelong learning.

The librarians of the four UC Access Colleges are proposing the incorporation of information literacy competencies into the Freshman English curriculum. By providing a standardized, course-integrated curriculum, the faculty can be assured that their students will be taught the fundamental skills and concepts needed to successfully complete their research assignments.

The focus of the lectures will be upon critical-thinking skills required to select and synthesize information. This will be accomplished by instructing students how to select, use and evaluate resources, databases, and services offered by the University libraries. Specific competencies to be included:

1. Understanding the organization and structure of information
    by describing and defining the variety and scope of resources
    by explaining the structure of resources offered at UC
2. Articulating information needs
    by formulating the research question
    by identifying key words
3. Locating and retrieving resources
    by identifying and using relevant resources
    by developing an appropriate research strategy
    by retrieving the resources within the University libraries
    by retrieving resources external to the University libraries
4. Evaluating resources to select appropriate information
    by use of multiple evaluating criteria including: currency, authority, bias, intended audience, accuracy
    by distinguishing between scholarly and popular resources
5. Using information appropriately
    by citing information sources accurately

To ensure the successful instruction of these concepts and skills listed above, we recommend the following:
• two different fifty-minute lectures, one in Freshman English I and one in Freshman English II
• the use of demonstrations, hands-on class time, and multimedia presentations to enhance the didactic lectures
• the development of research assignments that incorporate information literacy competencies

We are very willing to work with and assist the faculty in developing the information literacy curriculum and research assignments that will meet the instructional goals and objectives. We believe that the instruction of critical-thinking skills to locate and evaluate information resources is a joint responsibility of librarians and professors.

Stephena Harmony, RWC Library; Fred Marcotte, Clermont College Library; Debra Oswald, RWC Library; and Rosemary Young, OMI CAS Library. Reprinted with permission.

Librarians who get involved in their institutions' curriculum committee may gain the necessary political clout for institution-wide recognition of the importance of information literacy competencies. From this position, librarians can address the issue of incorporating library skills and information management education within the curriculum. If librarians are not permitted to serve on the institution's curriculum committee, try to obtain status as a consultant to the curriculum committee.

Librarians are making inroads in establishing information literacy as a required skill for life through the bottom-up approach laid out in this chapter. It is significant that information literacy competency requirements have made their way into some standards established by accrediting agencies.[10] This top-down pressure will lend fuel to information literacy efforts.

NOTES

1. P. Steven, Bibliographic Instruction Listserv, listserv@listserv.byu. edu; posted September 16, 1996.
2. Bethany Lawton, "Library Instruction Needs Assessment: Designing Survey Instruments," *Research Strategies* 7 (summer 1989): 119–128.
3. Patricia Daragan and Gwendolyn Stevens, "Developing Lifelong Learners," *Research Strategies* 14 (1996): 68–81.
4. Lawton, "Library Instruction Needs Assessment," p. 119.
5. *Ibid.*, pp. 119–128.
6. D.W. Stewart and P.N. Sharndasarri, *Focus Groups: Theory and Practice* (Newbury Park, CA: Sage, 1990), p. 414.
7. Trudi E. Jacobson and John R. Vallely, "A Half-built Bridge: The Unfinished Work of Bibliographic Instruction," *The Journal of Academic Librarianship* 17 (1992): 359–363.
8. Kari Boyd McBride and Ruth Dickstein, "The Web Demands Critical Reading by Students," *The Chronicle of Higher Education* (March 20, 1998): B6+.
9. Craig Gibson, "Accountability for BI Programs in Academic Libraries: Key Issues for the 1990s," in *Assessment & Accountability in Reference Work*, ed. S. G. Blandy, et al. (New York: Haworth, 1992), p. 103.
10. Middle States Commission on Higher Education, *Characteristics of Excellence in Higher Education: Standards for Accreditation*, (Philadelphia: MAS/CHE, 1994), p. 15.

SUGGESTED FURTHER READING

The following provide excellent examples of faculty assessment surveys.

Cannon, Anita. "Faculty Survey on Library Research Instruction." *RQ* 33 (4) (summer 1994): 524–41.

LaGuardia, Cheryl, Michael Blake, Lawrence Dowler, Laura Farwell, Caroline M. Kent, and Ed Tallent. *Teaching the New Library: A How-To-Do-It Manual for Planning and Designing Instructional Programs.* (New York: Neal-Schuman, 1996), pp. 40–43.

Lawton, Bethany. "Library Instruction Needs Assessment: Designing Survey Instruments." *Research Strategies,* 7 (3) (summer 1989): 119–128. (This includes surveys for faculty, staff, and students.)

Maynard, J. Edmund. "A Case Study of Faculty Attitudes toward Library Instruction: The Citadel Experience." *Reference Services Review* 18 (summer 1990): 67–76.

Thomas, Joy. "Faculty Attitudes and Habits Concerning Library Instruction: How Much Has Changed Since 1982." *Research Strategies* 12 (4) (fall 1994): 209–223.

3 COURSE-INTEGRATED INSTRUCTION

Francesca Allegri has defined course-integrated instruction (CII) as "instruction which meets at least three of the following four criteria: 1) faculty outside the library are involved in the design, execution and evaluation of the program, 2) the instruction is curriculum-based, in other words, directly related to the students' course work and/or assignments, 3) students are required to participate, and 4) the student's work is graded or credit is received for participation."[1] To many librarians involved in instruction, this describes an ideal situation. It is well documented that when a student is taught a skill at the "teachable moment"— that moment in time when the skill is required and the student is receptive—the skill is more likely to be learned. Course-integrated library instruction ideally is providing librarians with the perfect "teachable moment."

Unfortunately, reality may differ somewhat from the ideal. For example, instructors may schedule the library-skills class on a day when they plan to be out of town for a conference. This may be convenient for the instructor, but the teachable moment may be lost if students do not have a clear understanding of their research assignment or their chosen topic. The timing of the library-skills class is an important issue that should be discussed with the instructor. Students are receptive to information when they need that information, not a week or two before they understand how they might apply the skills you are teaching.

Though instruction on library skills for Freshman English research papers may be some librarians' worst nightmare, it offers an important opportunity to make the library's first impression on freshmen that could affect their interactions with the library their entire academic careers. This opportunity to interact with the majority of incoming freshmen is your time to make that interaction productive and useful; it is your start toward creating information literate library users.

The Freshman English class is just one example of course-integrated instruction. How can this class and others be changed from a class dreaded by both student and librarian to a valuable, teachable moment? To accomplish this, return to Allegri's definition of course-integrated instruction, which will be used for the purposes of this book. Allegri points to the need for faculty involvement throughout the process but also recognizes the need for mandatory student participation and the use of graded assignments.

FACULTY INVOLVEMENT IN DESIGN OF COURSE-INTEGRATED INSTRUCTION

The importance of faculty participation in preparation for course integrated instruction cannot be overemphasized. Faculty cannot be expected to keep current on what is new in the library, so librarians need to take the time to discuss with faculty the latest resources that can be of use to their students. Involve the faculty in making informed decisions on which library skills and resources should be taught to their students—keeping a realistic eye on what can be introduced in the time allowed. It is possible that if the faculty member comprehends the vastness of the amount of information you are being asked to cover and students to absorb in fifty minutes, that you may get more time alotted to introduce skills to the students. If you have been successful with educating faculty members, as described in Chapter 2, then you are more likely to be successful in your endeavor to involve faculty in designing CII programs.

FACULTY INVOLVEMENT IN EXECUTION OF COURSE-INTEGRATED INSTRUCTION

As we have noted, the timing of introducing library skills is important—using the teachable moment. Students are receptive to the introduction of new skills when they realize that they need them for an assignment. If the criterion for the timing of the class is when the instructor is unavailable to be in the classroom, that valuable teachable moment is lost. If CII is to teach students the research skills necessary to complete a research paper assignment, then students must come to the training with their topics articulated and ready to begin their research.

The presence of the teacher in the classroom is important. In fact, the librarian should require not just their presence but also their participation. Librarian/faculty team teaching in a graduate environment is common in research courses. Librarian/faculty team teaching in an undergraduate environment is less common, but no less important. Students take their cues from their professors, valuing information that the professor deems important. Team teaching lends legitimacy to the information being presented by the librarian. When a librarian makes a point in the classroom and the instructor follows this up with

Figure 3.1   Faculty Evaluation of Library Instruction

Name _____ Class _____

Librarian _____ No. of Students _____ Date _____

Presentation skills:
Organization of subject matter presented

Needs improvement   1   2   3   4   5   6   7   8   9   10   Excellent

Speaking skills

Needs improvement   1   2   3   4   5   6   7   8   9   10   Excellent

Use of active learning techniques

Needs improvement   1   2   3   4   5   6   7   8   9   10   Excellent

Encouraged questions from students

Needs improvement   1   2   3   4   5   6   7   8   9   10   Excellent

Content:
Covered material appropriate for class assignment

Needs improvement   1   2   3   4   5   6   7   8   9   10   Excellent

Used appropriate examples

Needs improvement   1   2   3   4   5   6   7   8   9   10   Excellent

Provided strategy for approaching research assignment

Needs improvement   1   2   3   4   5   6   7   8   9   10   Excellent

Supporting materials:
Relevancy of handouts

Needs improvement   1   2   3   4   5   6   7   8   9   10   Excellent

What changes/improvements would you suggest for future classes?

Was the computer demonstration effective in your opinion? Why/Why not?

Would you use this service again? Why/Why not?

Additional comments? (please use back of form)

an explanation on how this is important to the student on their next homework assignment, students take notice.

FACULTY INVOLVEMENT IN EVALUATION OF COURSE-INTEGRATED INSTRUCTION

Faculty should be involved in evaluating both the librarian's teaching effectiveness and student learning in CII programs. When evaluating the librarian, the emphasis must be on developing teaching skills and providing suggestions for improvement. It is strongly advised that these evaluations be used not in performance reviews but only to contribute to improvements in teaching performance. (This will be discussed further in Chapter 6.) Figure 3.1 offers a sample faculty questionnaire for evaluating librarians' teaching effectiveness.

Faculty must also be involved in the evaluation of student learning. This evaluation should be accomplished through grading a mandatory assignment that incorporates the skills taught in the library class. The librarian and faculty member should create the assignment together, basing it on the faculty member's goals for the library component of the course, and both should grade it. A more detailed discussion of the assignment is provided later in this chapter.

Many faculty have found that "course integrated library skills instruction has a positive impact on student's mastery both of subject matter content and of information seeking skills."[2] With faculty involvement at all stages of course-integrated instruction, faculty will see this impact.

COURSE-RELATED COVERAGE

Course-integrated instruction is meant to be curriculum based and directly related to the student's course work and assignments. The Freshman English curriculum at the University of Cincinnati College of Applied Science emphasizes technical writing skills. The research process as presented in the library-skills class is directly related to the research-paper assignment that culminates their quarter's work. Figure 3.2 provides an outline for a CII program for Freshman English in which both concepts and skills are emphasized. Students look at types of periodical publications and determine what would be appropriate sources for research for academic papers or on the job. There is a

---

FIGURE 3.2 Outline for Freshman English Library Research Presentation

1. What is a periodical?

2. What kinds of periodical publications are there?
   (Refer to handout and exercise in distinguishing scholarly/trade journals and general interest/popular magazines)

3. Why are periodical publications important to you in school and in your future career?

4. How do you access information in periodicals?

5. What different kinds of indexes are available?

6. Strategies for searching indexes:
   identifying keywords

   Boolean logic operators

   truncation

   proximity searching

   (Emphasis placed on transferability of these strategies to all databases)

7. Importance and use of help screens and information screens.

8. Demonstration of a general periodicals database and a specialized database using the search statement developed by students.

broad overview of searching strategies so students can transfer their use from one database to another. The class emphasizes the use of information screens and help screens, as students will find these useful when doing research for other classes in other databases.

During the class, the specific tools that the faculty member requested are demonstrated. Students have an opportunity to discuss the different types of articles retrieved from these databases and the appropriate use of popular magazine articles and scholarly journal articles.

The class uses active learning methods throughout. Students are engaged in answering the questions posed in the outline in Figure 3.2. Samples of popular/general interest magazines and scholarly/trade journals are at each student table. As they review a handout that lists criteria for differentiating scholarly from nonscholarly periodicals (see Figure 3–3), students examine their samples and identify what type of publications they have in hand.

After students are introduced to types of periodical publications, there is extensive discussion of the number and types of indexes available that provide subject access to articles in periodicals. Following this exercise, a sample research topic is posed. Students at the College of Applied Science are encouraged to choose technical topics for their Freshman English research papers, usually in their area of study. Research topics cover topics such as the Y2K problem, indoor air quality, safety techniques in the construction industry, high-speed machining, and the like. One of these topics is generally chosen for the demonstration.

Next, students identify the appropriate keywords. They must expand on the keywords by suggesting synonyms or singular or plural versions of the keywords. For example, if the topic is "indoor air quality," an appropriate synonym might be "sick building syndrome."

Once an appropriate list of keywords has been identified, strategies for searching indexes are introduced. As truncation and Boolean logic operators are presented, students choose how to put together the search statement using these strategies with their keyword list. They then use a handout that lists the databases available to them to identify ones that would be appropriate for their research. They search in both a general periodicals database that indexes popular/general interest magazines and some scholarly/trade journals, and an applied sciences database that indexes only scholarly/trade journals. The students then compare the citations retrieved from each database and discuss which database is the most appropriate source for information for their research-paper assignment for this class, for other classes, or on the job.

Figure 3.3   Distinguishing Scholarly from Nonscholarly Periodicals

This guide lists criteria to help you identify scholarly journals, trade journals, and magazines. It is the first step in critically evaluating your source of information.

SCHOLARLY JOURNAL

Reports original research or experimentation.

Articles written by an expert in the field for other experts in the field.

Articles use specialized jargon of the discipline.

Articles undergo peer review process before acceptance for publication in order to assure creative content.

Authors of articles always cite their sources in the form of footnotes or bibliographies.

> **Examples of scholarly journals:**
> *The International Journal of Applied Engineering Education*
> *Journal of the Association for Computing Machinery*
> *Journal of Organizational Behavior*

TRADE JOURNAL

Discusses practical information in industry.

Contains business news, product information, advertising, and trade articles.

Contains information on current trends in technology.

Articles usually written by experts in the field for other experts in the field.

Articles use specialized jargon of the discipline.

Useful to people in the trade field and to people seeking orientation to a vocation.

> **Examples of trade journals:**
> *Aviation Week and Space Technology*
> *Chemical Marketing Reporter*
> *Professional Engineer*

GENERAL-INTEREST MAGAZINE

Provides information in a general manner to a broad audience.

Articles generally written by a member of the editorial staff or a freelance writer.

Language of articles geared to any educated audience, no subject expertise assumed.

Articles are often heavily illustrated, generally with photographs.

No peer review process.

Sources are sometimes cited, but more often there are no footnotes or bibliography.

> **Examples of general interest magazines:**
> *Newsweek*
> *Psychology Today*
> *Popular Electronics*   **(continued)**

Figure 3.3 (continued)

POPULAR MAGAZINE

Articles are short and written in simple language with little depth to the content of these articles.

The purpose is generally to entertain, not necessarily to inform.

Information published in popular magazines is often second- or third-hand.

The original source of information contained in articles is obscure.

Articles are written by staff members or freelance writers.

Examples of popular magazines:
People
Reader's Digest

Note: You can find more information about periodical titles by consulting Bill and Linda Sternberg Katz's *Magazines for Libraries* 9th ed., R.R. Bowker, 1997, (Reference Z6941.M23) or Gail Skidmore's *From Radical Left to Extreme Right: a Bibliography of Current Periodicals* 3rd ed., Metuchen, NJ., Scarecrow, 1987.

TRANSFERABILITY OF SKILLS TAUGHT

By definition, course-integrated instruction is curriculum based. An important component of CII however, is that its skills are transferable.

Faculty requests to demonstrate a specific research tool should not deter you from also making sure the students gain a broad understanding of information-seeking skills. If the faculty member is well schooled in the rapidly changing environment of library research, you will likely not have a problem incorporating this concept.

For example, the University of Cincinnati College of Applied Science is a baccalaureate college that specializes in teaching engineering technologies. The students prefer to be taught practical applications over theory, tools rather than concepts. However, the library's most successful classes, both in terms of reception by students and successful completion of assignments, include a healthy mix of both concepts and specific tools. This approach makes the students and faculty happy because they are introduced to the specific tools they require as well as to concepts that will serve them in a multitude of classes. Remember to emphasize transferability of the skills and concepts being learned to other databases, to other classes, and to future jobs.

As one example of emphasizing transferability of skills, the Freshman English library-skills classes point out that search strategies such as truncation, adjacency searching, and Boolean logic operators work in all databases but are presented in a different manner from database to database. For example, the truncation symbol in one database may be a "?" but in another database it may be a "*." This is a good instance to demonstrate the usefulness of help screens, so the students understand that each database they will get has this information.

MANDATORY GRADED ASSIGNMENT

The practical application of concepts and skills introduced in a CII program should immediately follow presentations. This reinforces skills and encourages early interactions among the students and library staff. Students should complete a library assignment that will be graded, as ones that are not mandatory and graded are rarely given the attention they require.

The librarian and faculty member should develop and grade the assignment together. The following are tips for effective library assignments:

- Library assignments should be directly related to the course subject matter. This will help the student to master the subject matter as well as library skills, and give the student a concrete purpose for applying research skills.
- Students must understand the purpose of the project and how it will benefit them.
- The assignment should be a progressive project, with time and opportunity for feedback from both the librarian and faculty member.
- Library assignments should help the student to understand the transferability of library research skills from one research project to another.[3]

The Freshman English class described earlier in this chapter uses two assignments. The first is a short, two-page, graded assignment that reinforces the material covered in class. This is especially important when library-skills classes are taught in classrooms that do not provide hands-on computer time for the students. This short assignment gives the students an opportunity to follow the steps taught in class using their own research topic. Students can consult with their instructor and the librarian, and any students who fail the assignment are given an opportunity to resubmit it. The consultation and resubmission are meant to ensure that students learn library research techniques. It is also hoped that after this exercise students will find using the library less intimidating for the remainder of their academic career.

FIGURE 3.4   Library Exercise on Finding Information in Periodicals

Name: _____

Class (Time and Session): _____

1.   What is your major?:

2.   List three journals (either trade journals or scholarly journals) in your field of study:

   _____

   _____

   _____

3.   List two indexes to periodical literature that would be useful to you in your field of study and available at the library:

   _____

   _____

4.   Choose a topic of interest to you in a technical area. This should be the topic you choose for your research paper. Describe your topic in a complete sentence (for example: Do helmets protect motorcyclists?).

   _____

   _____

5.   List the KEYWORDS from your sentence above (in the above example, the KEYWORDS would be HELMETS and MOTORCYCLISTS):

   _____

   _____

6.   Are there variations on your KEYWORDS that you should use in your search, such as synonyms for your KEYWORDS, or singular or plural terms? If so, list those here (using the above example, your list would include words such as HELMET, HELMETS, HEADGEAR, MOTORCYCLIST, MOTORCYCLISTS, MOTORCYCLE, MOTORCYCLES, MOTORCYCLING):

   _____

   _____

7. Using search strategies demonstrated in class, write out your search statement using **Boolean logic operators** (AND, OR), **truncation** (*), or **parenthesis**, as appropriate. In the above example, a search statement would read: **(headgear or helmet*) and motorcycl***

   _____

   _____

8. Choose an appropriate periodical index to search for your topic. Use the handout "OhioLINK Database Overview" to make this selection.

   _____

   _____

   Why is this your best choice? _____

9. Using the search strategy which you created in Question #7, do a KEYWORD search for your topic of interest in the index you identified in Question #8.

   From the list of articles that you retrieve from your search, choose those articles that look like they will provide appropriate information on your topic.

   Print out the bibliographic citations for three articles you identify as appropriate, and attach these to this assignment.

10. Look at the full bibliographic record for the articles you chose above. Examine the subjects in the records and list the subject headings that are relevant to your topic.

    _____

    _____

11. Do a new search, this time a SUBJECT search, using the subject headings you listed above. Are you finding more relevant articles on your topic? Yes_____ No_____

12. Print out the bibliographic citations for three articles from the search you did in Question #11. Attach these to this assignment.

Figure 3.4 shows the short library assignment created for the freshman English class.

The second assignment is the research paper itself. This is a progressive assignment with multiple opportunities for feedback. The librarian provides feedback on the library-research portion of the paper by reviewing the students' annotated bibliographies for their research paper. The annotations, which must include evaluation of the information retrieved, are assessed using the following criteria:

- Were appropriate sources searched?
- Did the literature search capture appropriate literature on the topic?
- Did the annotation include a comparison of the views held by different authorities?
- Did the student give an evaluation of sources?

COURSE-INTEGRATED INSTRUCTION IN A PROFESSIONAL DEVELOPMENT COURSE

The above discussion concentrated on a Freshman English, course-integrated instruction experience, but CII concepts can be used in any course. At the College of Applied Science, the librarian teaches a library skills class to all professional development (PD) classes on how to access information. Developed jointly by the professional practice faculty and the librarian, the instruction is curriculum based.

The professional development course teaches students how to write a resume, how to interview, and a variety of other skills necessary to identify a job in their field and get hired. Representatives from industries that routinely employ the college's graduates speak to the students about what skills they are looking for in their new hires. The librarian's lecture dovetails with the curriculum, providing students with the skills to identify companies in their field and do in-depth research on these companies. The students use these skills to find cooperative education jobs and, eventually, their permanent positions upon graduation. Faculty are involved in the execution and the evaluation of the program. Students in the professional development class are required to participate, and there is a graded assignment.

Figure 3.5 shows an outline of the PD CII program. Students are actively involved in the class by providing names of companies of interest to them. These companies are then used by the librarian as search examples in the various databases demonstrated. Figure 3-6 shows

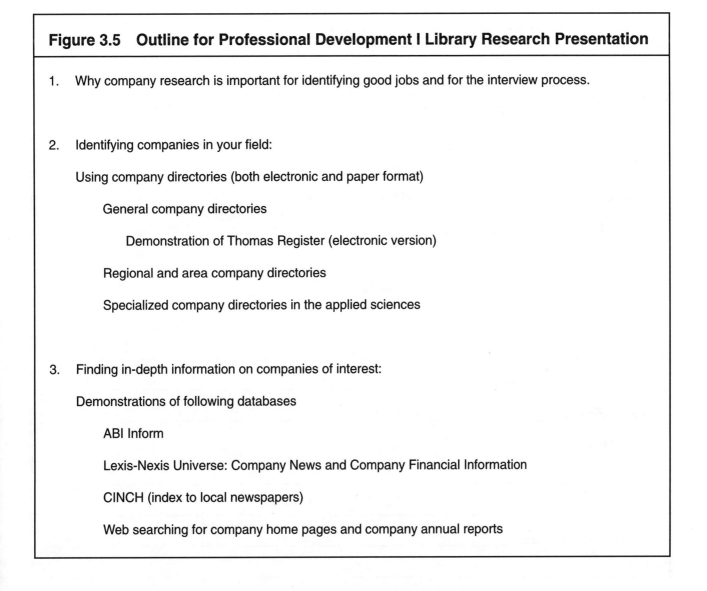

Figure 3.5   Outline for Professional Development I Library Research Presentation

1.   Why company research is important for identifying good jobs and for the interview process.

2.   Identifying companies in your field:

Using company directories (both electronic and paper format)

General company directories

Demonstration of Thomas Register (electronic version)

Regional and area company directories

Specialized company directories in the applied sciences

3.   Finding in-depth information on companies of interest:

Demonstrations of following databases

ABI Inform

Lexis-Nexis Universe: Company News and Company Financial Information

CINCH (index to local newspapers)

Web searching for company home pages and company annual reports

Figure 3.6   Company Research Assignment

Name: _____

Class Time: _____

Professor: _____

Name of company you have chosen to research: _____

Location(s)—local, regional, national, and international facilities:

_____

_____

Contact person (name, title, phone number, address): _____

_____

_____

Date company was established: _____

Type of industry: _____

Products/services: _____

_____

_____

New products/services: _____

_____

_____

Has the company shown substantial and consistent growth? Is the company expanding or retrenching? __

_____

_____

Who are the company's primary customers? _____

_____

Who are the company's major competitors? _____

_____

_____

Does the company have an established coop program? _____

If yes, what type of coop positions are available? _____

_____

_____

Why would you be interested in working with this organization? What skills, education, abilities do you currently have that would be relevant to this company? _____

_____

_____

List two sources from which you obtained information for this assignment. (One must be electronic and the second source may be from a paper or electronic source): _____

_____

the mandatory assignment, which is graded by both the librarian and the professional practice faculty member. Most questions require the use of library resources, although some are answered using materials in the professional practice suite. A cooperative collection-development program keeps both the library and professional practices departments well informed of available resources and makes student referrals easier.

Students are enthusiastic about this class. They can easily see how the research skills presented in this CII program will directly benefit them in future job searches.

SUMMARY

Course-integrated instruction offers librarians opportunities to forge lasting partnerships with faculty. It also offers unique opportunities to introduce life-long learning skills to students. Careful planning and collaboration between librarians and faculty can relieve the frustrations felt by many librarians attempting to teach research skills to an undergraduate population.

NOTES

1. Francesa Allegri, "Course Integrated Instruction: Metamorphosis for the Twenty-First Century," *Medical Reference Services Quarterly* 4 (winter 1985): 47–66.
2. Ross Todd, "Integrated Information Skills Instruction," *School Library Media Quarterly* 23 (winter 1995): 133–8.
3. Emily L. Werrell and Therasa Wesley, "Promoting Information Literacy Through a Faculty Workshop," *Research Strategies* 8 (fall 1990): 172–180.

4 NONINTEGRATED INSTRUCTION

Although the focus of this book is upon collaborating with faculty to provide course-integrated instruction, we cannot overlook nonintegrated teaching (stand-alone or one-time presentations provided by librarians, with no or little faculty involvement) as another opportunity to introduce students to information-research concepts. True, this method of instruction is not the ideal way to instill lifelong learning skills into undergraduates. However, it may be your only recourse within your institution. This chapter discusses the challenges in developing and delivering one-time lectures and stand-alone presentations that will gain faculty support and that will introduce students to the essential concepts of information literacy at the time that they need it.

DISTINCTION BETWEEN NONINTEGRATED AND COURSE-INTEGRATED INSTRUCTION

As defined in Chapter 3, course-integrated instruction must include at least three of the four following criteria: (1) the teaching faculty actively collaborate with the librarian to design, instruct, and evaluate the presentation content and assignments; (2) the instruction is curriculum based; (3) students are required to participate; and (4) students receive credit or grades for their participation (see page 29).[1] Nonintegrated instruction, however, is not an essential component to any specific course and/or research assignment. Although there may be some involvement between a faculty member and the librarian in deciding upon the content or in linking the presentation to a particular assignment, nonintegrated instruction lacks two essential criteria to qualify as course-integrated instruction: first, the faculty member does not actively collaborate with the librarian in designing and providing the content; second, the librarian usually has no or very little involvement in the design and evaluation of the research assignment.

METHODS OF PROVIDING NONINTEGRATED INSTRUCTION

Nonintegrated instruction encompasses two major methods: the stand-alone presentation, and the one-time classroom lecture. Stand-alone instruction sessions are scheduled and provided by librarians independent of academic course schedules and assignments. The librarians identify the topics and develop the sessions based upon their assessment of what students need to know and learn (such as introduction to the library's online catalog; general or subject specific databases and resources; or specialized topics such as career or financial aide resources). Students attend voluntarily, and do not receive assignments, credit, or grades for their participation.

In the case of the one-time lecture, the librarian is invited into the classroom by the faculty member. Usually there is some direction from the faculty member to the librarian on what to cover and whether to focus upon specific resources or research strategies to prepare students to begin work on a particular class assignment. The timing of the library presentation is at the discretion of the faculty and not necessarily at the teachable moment when the student is prepared to listen and learn. If there is a class assignment connected to the one-time presentation, the librarian rarely has any involvement in the design of the assignment or in the assessment of the students' work.

DEVELOPING AND MAINTAINING A SUCCESSFUL NONINTEGRATED INSTRUCTION PROGRAM

One-time lectures and stand-alone presentations are inadequate forums in which to teach students the full range of information literacy skills. In fact, one could argue that, aside from instructing students in the basic "mechanical" skills of what resources are available and how to perform simple searches, it is impossible to include the evaluation and problem-solving components of information literacy instruction in a fifty-minute lecture with no follow-up evaluation. The question then becomes; Why utilize this method in the first place? The answer for many of us is that the one-time classroom lecture may be our only option. Or, there may be only a small group of faculty with whom we can collaborate in developing course-integrated instruction and that we have not yet been able to extend this instruction throughout our institution.

Given these circumstances, you will need to address the following issues to create and maintain nonintegrated presentations that faculty will regularly request:

- gaining faculty support and input in planning the library-skills lecture and in identifying topics for the stand-alone presentations
- promoting the scope and availability of classroom and stand-alone presentations to faculty
- creating incentives for faculty support and student participation.

GAINING FACULTY SUPPORT AND INVOLVEMENT

When planning the one-time classroom lecture, engage the faculty member in a detailed discussion that goes beyond the five-minute phone call about the date, time, and a list of resources to cover. Ask the faculty member to describe how the library lecture will support the course objectives. Request a copy of the syllabus and, if there is time, review the textbooks or required readings to get a sense of the content. Try to gather more specific details from the faculty member such as:

- types of resources to cover, such as books, journals, Internet
- particular resources to be included
- detailed description or a list of topics for the research assignment
- additional concepts to include such as research strategies, evaluation of resources
- when the assignment will be due
- criteria that the faculty member will apply when grading the research assignment.

Not only will this discussion provide you with the content to include in the presentation, but it will inform the faculty member as to the scope of what is possible to cover. This is also your opportunity to recommend the inclusion of some of the key information literacy concepts that the faculty member might not otherwise request. It is a good idea to ask the faculty member to prioritize the three or four most important concepts and/or resources that should be included in the classroom presentation. This will help you achieve two important objectives: (1) clarification of what the faculty member deems important; and (2) involvement of the faculty member in designing the lecture content.

For stand-alone presentations, faculty input, though more problematic to obtain, will make it possible for you to design sessions that are relevant, even though they are not integrated into specific courses or research assignments. You may want to survey specific departments about the kinds of library-research projects that will be assigned and when these assignments will be made. Use this information to identify common areas upon which to focus (for example, types of resources, research strategies for a specific discipline) as well as to schedule the stand-alone sessions at those "teachable moments" during the quarter or semester.

PROMOTING THE SCOPE AND AVAILABILITY

Because of the voluntary nature of stand-alone presentations and the invitation aspect of one-time classroom lectures, you need to vigorously promote the availability of these instructional services to your faculty in order to reach as many students as possible. When planning your promotional materials and communications, utilize a variety of methods to inform your faculty. Disseminate your promotional materials at those critical moments when faculty are likely to be receptive (such as in the month before classes begin, when faculty are usually developing the course syllabus and assignments), as well as throughout the year. Seek advice from your college public-relations department on how to design attention-grabbing promotional materials. Create a unique identity through the use of a distinctive logo.

Five Additional Avenues of Promotion

In addition to using departmental meetings, new faculty orientations, brown-bag seminars, and faculty development workshops as discussed in Chapter 2, try promoting your instructional program in one or more of the following ways.

1. Brochures
- Include descriptions of the instructional modules and indicate the amount of time to present each one.
- Emphasize your ability to customize the classroom lecture to meet specific course assignments.
- Stress the importance of including the evaluation and effective use of information in addition to demonstrating the online catalog and specific research databases.
- Give instructions on how the faculty member may request classroom presentations.
- Provide guidelines to faculty on designing library-research assignments that will introduce students to important information literacy concepts.

2. Web sites
- Transfer your print brochures (as described above) into your Web site and include an online request form for classroom lectures.
- Include links to your tutorials to illustrate the availability of and easy access to resources that faculty can incorporate into their course assignments.
- Provide sample library assignments that you and/or other faculty have designed (with their permission).

3. Faculty and student handbooks
- Include your policies on providing your instructional services in the faculty handbook (see Chapter 8 on developing policies).
- In the student handbook describe the benefits to students in terms that will appeal to them (including saving time, improving grades).

4. In-house publications
- Contribute regularly to your college and student in-house print and electronic newsletters.

5. Reference desk follow-up
- Follow up with faculty whose library-research assignments appear to be difficult for the students to complete because they do not know how to use the resources to locate the information—or because the library does not provide the resources that support the assignment.
- Follow up with faculty who have distributed outdated library guides or instructional materials to inform them of your new and improved resources.

Remember to include part-time faculty in your efforts to promote your instructional program. Many colleges are hiring greater numbers of part-time faculty to provide a significant amount of instruction, especially for core courses such as Freshman English. It may not be easy to reach the part-time faculty through the normal channels that are effective with the full-time faculty, so contact department chairs to find out how they communicate with their part-time faculty and utilize these additional avenues of communication.

CREATING INCENTIVES FOR FACULTY AND STUDENT PARTICIPATION

Remember the old saying that you can lead a horse to water but can't make it drink? So it is with creating and promoting your instructional program for nonintegrated classroom and stand-alone presentations.

You need to create incentives that will spur the faculty to request classroom lectures and to encourage their students to attend the stand-alone presentations. Quite frankly, there are not many enticing promises at your disposal, especially for the stand-alone sessions. Thus, your powers of persuasion and creativity, coupled with a few tangible awards, are what you have to work with to convince faculty to support your instructional services. The strategies that you use to communicate these services are important factors in encouraging faculty to contact you about arranging classroom lectures. In essence, you must establish your credibility and demonstrate your trustworthiness to the faculty. The more visible you are within your college by actively participating in academic activities and committees, the more likely your faculty will perceive you as being a colleague.

Some students may be motivated to attend popular sessions—such as ones on the Internet—on their own time and volition. But if you can get the faculty to offer extra credit as an incentive for students who attend basic presentations on the online catalog or an introduction to research strategies, you will see a much stronger turnout. For, although in theory and on paper offering stand-alone sessions looks good, in practice the amount of effort and time you must spend to develop, promote, and offer these sessions may not result in the level of attendance to make it worth your while. In fact, for librarians in small academic libraries, we do not recommend you provide stand-alone sessions on a regular basis as a primary method of instructing students.

EIGHT RECOMMENDATIONS FOR DESIGNING THE CONTENT

Listed below are recommendations to consider as you design the content for the nonintegrated presentations.

1. Avoid the "canned" presentation for the classroom lecture, because students will not make the connection between a general overview and their specific class assignment.
2. Customize the stand-alone presentations through search examples that will engage the students' attention; consider using popular culture, major campus issues, or community concerns.
3. Involve the students through active class participation (see Chapter 3).

4. Distribute instructional handouts and refer to them throughout your presentation; students will focus upon your presentation rather than taking notes.
5. Provide hands-on practice, when possible, to reinforce learning.
6. Distribute written copies of the examples you use during your demonstration so that students can follow along.
7. If the class is large (more than twelve), ask the faculty member or another librarian to assist when providing hands-on instruction.
8. Emphasize the availability of reference assistance in the library; encourage students to schedule an appointment if they need additional help.

Figure 4–1 gives a sample outline of a one-time presentation lecture developed by the librarians at Raymond Walters College (Cincinnati) that introduces the university's online catalog, an electronic periodicals database, basic Internet searching, and a brief discussion on selecting subject headings. This two-hour lecture includes hands-on practice by the students in addition to live demonstrations by the librarian.

Figure 4.1   Outline For Library Research and Resources Presentation

CONTENT OUTLINE

5 minutes   Introduction and Overview
- Introduce yourself
- Describe what the session will cover
- Describe how the session will be helpful for class assignments

10 minutes   Selecting a Research Topic
- Suggest sources to get ideas for topics
- Discuss strategies on adjusting topic (e.g., narrowing/broadening)
- Describe the differences between subject headings and keywords

10 minutes   Finding Articles on a Subject
- Define periodicals
- Describe differences between scholarly journals and popular magazines
- Explain briefly variety of electronic databases

35 minutes   Infotrac Expanded Academic Index
- Describe what is included and how to access
- Demonstrate simple subject search (how to enter terms, how to interpret and select terms from subject list and subdivisions)
- Describe elements of a journal citation
- Describe Infotrac features (full-text, backfile, limit function)
- Hands-on exercise for simple subject search
- Explain and demonstrate Boolean search strategies
- Hands-on exercise for Boolean subject search

35 minutes   Finding Books in local and state online catalogs
- Describe your local & online catalogs
- Describe how to access from college workstations and dial-up/web procedures
- Demonstrate how to navigate through the catalog
- Demonstrate simple author and title searches
- Explain how to interpret screens (bibliographic information, holdings)
- Demonstrate how to request materials from other libraries in the network
- Hands-on exercise for author and title searches
- Reiterate differences between and demonstrate subject vs. keyword searching
- Hands-on exercise for subject and keyword searching

25 minutes   Searching the Internet
- Describe the variety and uncertainty of the quality of information
- Discuss the pros and cons of using Internet resources
- Describe basic navigation techniques of Internet browser (e.g., Netscape)
- Explain and demonstrate directories (e.g., Yahoo) and search engines (e.g., Hotbot)
- Hands-on exercise of simple Internet search

(continued)

Figure 4.1   (continued)

INSTRUCTIONAL HANDOUTS DISTRIBUTED TO STUDENTS TO SUPPLEMENT THE PRESENTATION
- Library guides for online catalogs
- Library guides describing general electronic periodicals databases (e.g., Expanded Academic Index, Periodicals Abstracts)
- Library guide describing services, hours, and telephone numbers
- "How to Evaluate Information" guide, which includes general criteria and specific issues when evaluating scholarly publications and the Internet
- Examples used in demonstrations throughout the presentation
- Hands-on exercises

TURNING NONINTEGRATED INSTRUCTION INTO AN OPPORTUNITY

Although nonintegrated instruction is not usually the preferred teaching method by librarians, it can offer a way to move toward course-integrated and collaborative partnerships with faculty. Some faculty may not be aware of the diversity and complexity of resources available through the library. Nor may they realize that the scope of these resources increases their students' difficulty in conducting research. Let your discussion with the faculty member achieve at least two additional objectives: educating the faculty on the necessity of incorporating information literacy skills into their course; and promoting your teaching ability.

Conducting short and simple evaluation surveys of both the students and faculty following your presentation will provide useful data in several areas. (See Figures 4.2 and 4.3 for examples.) First, you will receive feedback on how well the students understood the key concepts of your presentation and whether you need to revise the content or place more emphasis upon certain points. Second, the feedback you receive from the faculty should give you additional insight into the faculty member's perception of what the students need to learn. Third, following up at the end of the course will help you determine if the faculty member perceived improvements in the students' research assignments. Finally, sharing the student survey results may be very illuminating to the faculty member about how much (or how little) students know about conducting library research and what students think they need to know. These comments can be helpful in persuading the faculty member to request a course-integrated presentation, or could open the channels of communication to develop other collaborative teaching projects.

Figure 4.2   Library Instruction Student Evaluation

We would like to know what you thought of the library instruction session you just completed. Please circle your response. Thank you for taking part in this evaluation.

1.   Have you ever attended a library instruction session here before today?

no   yes   (If yes, note how many sessions you have attended here: _____)

2.   I have an idea of how to find books using the online catalog.

agree   unsure   disagree

3.   I have an idea of how to search for articles in Infotrac.

agree   unsure   disagree

4.   I know how to choose the best words or terms to find the information that I need.

agree   unsure   disagree

5.   I understand how to find information using the resources demonstrated in today's session.

agree   unsure   disagree

6.   Today's session will help me with my coursework for this class.

agree   unsure   disagree

7.   I have a better understanding of how the research process works because of today's session.

agree   unsure   disagree

8.   How would you improve this instruction session?

9.   What did you particularly like or appreciate about this instruction session?

Please feel free to make additional comments or suggestions below or on the back of this form.

Figure 4.3 Library Instruction Faculty Survey

Thank you for taking the time to complete this survey. Please return it to _____ at the library within one week from today.

Your department: _____

1. What was your primary reason for scheduling library instruction for your class?

2. Of the total number of classes that you teach, how many do you routinely bring to the library for an orientation or request an instruction session?

    a few   half   most   all

3. Did you find the material presented in the session useful to your students for working on their class assignment(s)?

    yes   no   unsure

4. Have you noticed an improvement in your students' research skills due to the instruction they received?

    yes   no   unsure

5. How would you improve our instruction session(s)?

6. What did you particularly like or appreciate about our instruction session(s)?

Please feel free to make additional comments or suggestions below or on the back of this form.

NOTE

1. Francesa Allegri, "Course Integrated Instruction: Metamorphosis for the Twenty-First Century," *Medical Reference Services Quarterly* 4 (winter 1985): 47–66.

ADDITIONAL RESOURCES

A number of libraries have created Web sites that include their instructional materials and services. Listed below are the URLs for three such sites.

University of Buffalo Oscar A. Silverman Undergraduate Library. To Arrange Library Library Instruction for a Class: ublib.buffalo.edu/libraries/units/ugl/bicover.html

UCLA College Library Instruction for UCLA Classes: www.library.ucla.edu/libraries/college/instruct/instucla.htm#how

University of Oregon Library Instruction: libweb.uoregon.edu/instruct/

5 FULL-CREDIT INFORMATION LITERACY COURSES

The time constraints imposed by the standard fifty-minute library skills presentation limits these to procedural explanations or demonstrations of specific library resources. There is little time to give students an appreciation of information and library resources in a broad social context. Full-credit information literacy courses allow time to develop the social context as a conceptual framework for instruction. Deborah Fink gives an in-depth look into developing such a social context in the book *Conceptual Frameworks for Bibliographic Instruction.*[1]

Fink points out that there are numerous advantages to establishing a social context for information literacy training.

- sparking student interest
- helping students understand that the skills they learn go beyond usefulness for their immediate assignment
- elevating information literacy-training from a skill set to part of the academic mainstream

This last point is especially important when developing a full-credit information literacy course. A full-credit course must offer content beyond teaching the "process" of finding information if it is to be valued and accepted by other teaching faculty.

Fink offers numerous examples of social contexts to frame a course around:

- the politics of information, including censorship, propaganda, and bias
- the impact of computer technology
- citizenship in the information society

This chapter outlines preliminary steps to take when considering a full-credit course. It also includes the outline for a three-credit-hour, quarter-long course.

PRELIMINARY STEPS

STEP 1. GET FACULTY SUPPORT

When considering developing a full-credit information literacy program, consult with faculty to discern their level of support. Remember that faculty control curriculum committees that approve new course offerings, that faculty advisors direct students to specific course offerings, and that the faculty will determine if the information literacy course is a requirement or elective in various majors. If faculty members perceive a need for students to be information literate, a full-credit information literacy course can be a successful offering.

Gaining faculty support for this endeavor, however, may be difficult. As Hardesty points out, "Faculty are valued for what they know rather than what they can help others learn."[2] The theoretician is more highly valued than the practitioner—an attitude that places librarians in a lower rank. Faculty place emphasis on content, not process. "Most believe that content or subject matter—not the process of finding information about the disciplines—is of primary importance."[3] If a curriculum committee thinks that a full-credit information literacy course is teaching only process and has no content beyond this, the committee could easily reject that course. This often frustrates librarians, as they understand the importance of teaching process.

To assess faculty views on full-credit information literacy course offerings, use the methods described in Chapter 2. Faculty surveys, individual interviews, or focus groups will help you find the answers to your questions on perceived need for such a program and possible course content.

STEP 2. GET LIBRARY SUPPORT

You also need the full support of the library administration in this effort. Does a full-credit course fit with the library's mission and goals? A full-credit offering requires a large commitment of time and money; will administration provide the necessary support, both personnel and equipment? Once you have ascertained faculty support for a full-credit course, develop a proposal to present to library administration that utilizes the results of your faculty survey and/or interviews to bolster your request.

STEP 3. DETERMINE COURSE LEVEL

Will the course be a lower-division class directed at students at the beginning of their academic career? Or will it target upper-division students requiring specialized and sophisticated searching tools and techniques? The results of your surveys and interviews should propel your decision.

STEP 4. DECIDE HOW MANY CREDIT HOURS TO GIVE

Determine the number of credit hours for the full-credit course. This is usually based on the number of hours that a class meets each week. The greater the course content, the greater the number of credit hours. Your institution's curriculum committee may be able to give you guidance in this matter.

COURSE OUTLINE, CONTENT, AND STRUCTURE

COURSE GOALS

The course plan must begin with clearly articulated goals. What knowledge and skills do you want your students to gain from taking the class? This should reflect not only your expectations of students, but faculty expectations as well.

Information literacy courses share some basic, common goals:

- to ensure students' abilities to articulate their information needs
- to enable students to select appropriate sources for their information needs
- to provide students with the skills to search and retrieve information from a variety of sources
- to give students the ability to evaluate resources.

In a full-credit course, there is time to develop a social context for information literacy. The conceptual framework you choose for presenting information literacy skills can be virtually anything. Deborah Fink suggests "the politics of information" as a provocative framework, which could include discussions of censorship, propaganda, bias, and the information rich and information poor.[4] Another choice could be the ethical implications of information technologies, which could include privacy in an information age, intellectual property, information security, and free and open access to government information.

Depending on the conceptual framework introduced in your full-credit course, there will be additional goals added to the above list. For example,

- aim to provide students with an understanding of the ethical implications of information technologies.

GRADING POLICIES

The grading policy must be clearly articulated and should be included in the syllabus (see Figure 5.1). As you develop the course content, you must decide if students will receive grades for homework assignments and classroom discussion and how to weight these grades compared to grades earned on exams, research papers, or research dossiers. The grading policy statement in the syllabus in Figure 5.1 shows that some homework assignments are graded and are given specific weight in considering the overall grade, but that others are not; to insure that students complete the work, however, all ungraded assignments count toward class participation.

Figure 5.1 Syllabus for Accessing and Evaluating Information for Lifelong Learning

INSTRUCTOR:

COURSE DESCRIPTION:
In order to function in the "information age," it is necessary to be information literate. Information literacy is the ability to locate, evaluate, and effectively use needed information. This course will engender these skills. The first goal of the course is to ensure that students have the skills to select appropriate sources for their information needs. A clear understanding of available resources is necessary to make appropriate selections. The second goal is to provide students with the skills to search and retrieve information from a variety of resources. Electronic resources will be emphasized. The third goal is to ensure that students have the ability to evaluate resources. Students will have the opportunity to access information on the World Wide Web and critically evaluate this information. The fourth goal is to provide the student with an understanding of the ethical implications of information technologies. The ethical aspects to be discussed are specifically: privacy in an information age; intellectual property; information security; and free and open access to electronic government information.

TEXTBOOKS:
The Elements of Information Gathering, by Donald Zimmerman (1995)
Evaluating Information, by Jeffrey Katzer et al. (3rd ed.) (1991)

ADDITIONAL READINGS:
Citizen Rights and Access to Electronic Information, edited by Dennis Reynolds (1992)
Ethical Aspects of Information Technology, by Richard Spinello (1995)
Information Anxiety, by Richard Saul Wurman (1990)
Information Literacy: Revolution in the Library, by Patricia Senn Breivik and E. Gordon Gee (1989)
Internet 101: A College Student's Guide, by Alfred Glossbrenner (1995)
Realizing the Information Future: The Internet and Beyond, by Computer Science and Telecommunications Board of the National Research Council (1994)
Using Government information Sources, by Jean Sears (1994)

Various articles as noted in the reading assignments. (All articles will be available on Reserve in the Library.)

COMMUNICATING:
Every student must sign up for a student online account if they do not already have one. Communications with the instructor will be possible via e-mail or office hours as posted at the beginning of the quarter.

GRADING POLICY:
Four homework assignments (5% each)	20%
Classroom discussions	10%
Three exams (20% each)	60%
Final paper	10%

90%–100%=A, 80%–89%=B, 70%–79%=C, 60%–69%=D, 0%–59%=F

Attendance and participation is required. Three or more unexcused absences will invoke a failing grade (F).

Participation in discussion is required of all students.

Assignments will not be accepted after the announced deadlines unless the student first obtains permission for the delay.

The instructor will collect ungraded assignments and will provide suggestions and guidance to the students on areas for improvement based on these assignments.

The three exams will be a combination of essay questions, hands-on searching skills assessments, and short answers.

The final paper will be on a topic of the student's choice from parameters set by the instructor. It will deal with some aspect of the impact of information technology. Please see attached grade sheet for evaluation method to be used for all written assignments.

CLASS SCHEDULE AND ASSIGNMENTS:
Week/Subject Material

WEEK 1

Class 1
Introductions; review of syllabus; assignments; grading policies; verification that every student has information to sign up for an online account.

Reading assignment:
Wurman, Chapters 1, 14

Class 2
Discussion of concepts of information literacy and the term "information age." Discussion of the need for information literacy in an "information age." Discussion on the impact of technologies on information from fax and e-mail to CD-ROM, OPACs, Internet, and the World Wide Web.

Writing assignment:
One page each on the following (ungraded assignment): (1) Define your own information-seeking behavior. (2) Survey two instructors on their information-seeking behavior and write about how they use information in their profession.

Class 3
Presentations by students on their information-seeking habits and those of their instructors. Discussion of information seeking habits required for success in an "information age."

Reading assignment:
Breivik and Gee, Chapter 2

WEEK 2

Class 4
Overview of the structure and form of recorded information. Discussion of primary and secondary resources.

Reading assignment:
Zimmerman, Chapters 3–4

Class 5
Overview of OPACs, CD-ROMs, Internet, full-text, hybrid, and bibliographic databases.

Reading assignment
Zimmerman, Chapters 5–6

Class 6
Introduction to terminology and concepts used to access information: subject headings, thesaurus, synonyms, controlled vocabulary, free-text searching, searching fields, search engines, keywords, citation, abstract, browsers, etc. In-class exercises in creating a thesaurus.

Writing assignment:
Create a thesaurus for topics handed out by instructor in class (ungraded assignment).

WEEK 3

Class 7
Introduction to Boolean logic operators, adjacency, truncation. Working with searching strategies. In-class exercises in creating search strategies for topics of the students choice.

Writing assignment:
Create possible search strategies for topics assigned by the instructor. This is due at the beginning of the next class (graded assignment).

Reading assignments:
J.A. Large, "Evaluating Online and CD-ROM Reference Sources," *Journal of Librarianship* 21 (2): 87–108 (1989).
E.P. Weston, "How Do We Learn What a Database Includes," *RQ* 28: 35–41 (1988).

Class 8
Discussion on evaluating information sources; criteria for evaluating database content. Selecting appropriate resources for specific information needs; needs assessment.

Class 9
First exam

Reading assignment:
Katzer, Chapters 1–3

WEEK 4

Class 10
Short discussion on the introductory chapters of Katzer's book on evaluating information. You will be reading Katzer's book over the next three weeks. The first two weeks of this period, you will be learning how to gather information electronically. The third week, we will discuss applying Katzer's criteria for evaluating information. Introduction to full-text databases: ABI Inform, Periodical Abstracts, Social Issues Resource Series. Application of the search strategies and other concepts used in accessing information will be discussed.

Reading assignment:
Katzer, Chapters 4–5

Class 11
Full-text databases: Lexis/Nexis Universe. Continuing discussion on evaluating information.

Reading assignment:
Katzer, Chapters 6–7

Writing assignment:
Compare Lexis/Nexis, ABI Inform, Periodicals Abstracts, and SIRS full-text databases using the criteria you learned from the articles by Large and Weston and from discussion in class 8. You have one week to complete this assignment. It will be due at class 14 (graded assignment).

Class 12
Discussion on "bias" and "noise" as introduced by Katzer.

Assignment:
Identify articles where you have seen examples of "bias" and "noise." Be prepared to discuss these at the next class.

Reading assignment:
Katzer, Chapters 8–9

WEEK 5

Class 13
Citation databases: Applied Science and Technology Index, NTIS. Students should have examples on where they have identified "bias" and "noise" in recent newspaper articles or other readings. Introduction to a numeric database: Compac Disclosure.

Searching assignment:
Perform a subject search in both ASTI and NTIS on topics provided by the instructor. Hand in the printouts of your search strategies and printouts of the first five citations resulting from your searches at the next class (ungraded assignment).

Writing assignment:
Each student must meet with the instructor this week during posted office hours to discuss the topic they have chosen for their final paper.

Reading assignment:
Katzer, Chapters 10–12

Class 14
Discussion on what a "table of contents service" is and how this service can aid in keeping current in your field. Each student will set up own profile to receive table of contents notices online.

Reading assignment:
Katzer, Chapters 13–15

Class 15
Evaluating information found in articles/books. By now, you should have read most of Katzer's book. We will begin in-depth discussions on the need to evaluate information and discuss the suggestions that Katzer has made in his book.

Reading assignment:
Katzer, Chapters 16–18

WEEK 6

Class 16
Discussion on applying Katzer's criteria as he presents them in Chapters 16–17.

Reading assignment:
P. Abelson, "Mechanisms for Evaluating Scientific Information and the Role of Peer Review," *Journal of the American Society for Information Science* 41 (3): 216–222 (1990).
S. J. Pierce, "Subject Areas, Disciplines, and the Concept of Authority," *LISR* 13: 21–35 (1991).

Class 17
Evaluating information: the importance of peer review of articles in scholarly journals; how to evaluate the author's authority. Scholarly and nonscholarly publications are discussed.

Writing assignment:
Using an article provided by the instructor, evaluate: the journal from which the article came; the article itself using Katzer's criteria; and the author's authority in the area in which they are writing. You have two weeks to complete this assignment—due at class 24 (graded assignment).

Class 18
Second exam

Reading assignment:
Reynolds, pages 39–44, 107–111, 175–177.

Writing assignment:
Each student must meet with the instructor this week during posted office hours to review their preliminary dossier for the final paper. It is expected that the dossier will be near completion at this point.

WEEK 7
Class 19
Government documents: issues for accessing government information in a free and democratic society.

Reading assignment:
Sears, Chapters 1–3

Class 20
Tour and orientation to government-documents collection at a depository library. Hands-on searching opportunities will be available.

Reading assignment:
Computer Science and Telecommunications Board, Chapters 1, 4

Class 21
Introduction to Internet and Web. Introduction to listservs, usenets, and electronic bulletin boards. Demonstration of how to sign onto listservs and usenets.

Writing assignment:
Use the Internet Yellow Pages (on reserve in the Library) or the Henderson article cited below to identify listservs and usenets appropriate to your college major. Sign onto two listservs or usenets of your choice. Monitor the information found on these listservs and write an evaluation of quality of information found through these sources. If you find that the listservs you are signed onto are not active enough to provide information to evaluate, sign onto other listservs. This assignment is due in one week (graded assignment).

Reading assignment:
Glossbrenner, Chapters 1–4
T. Henderson, "Major Links: the Internet is a Valuable Ally in the Study of Any Discipline," *Internet World* 6 (10): 50–54 (October 1995).

WEEK 8

Class 22
Search engines on the Web.

Reading assignment:
Glossbrenner, Chapters 5–7

Class 23
Research resources on the Web.

Reading assignment:
Glossbrenner, Chapters 12–14

Class 24
Discussion of quality and quantity of information found on the Internet. Presentations by students of the results of their assignment from class 21.

Reading assignment:
Spinello, Chapter 1

Writing assignment:
All students must meet with the instructor this week for a final review of the dossier and a preliminary look at the paper that is being developed.

WEEK 9

Class 25
Discussion on ethical aspects and security issues for information technology.

Reading assignment:
Spinello, Chapter 5

Class 26
Discussion on privacy in an information age.

Reading assignment:
Spinello, Chapters 6–7
R. L. Jacobson, "'Fair Use' Impasse," *The Chronicle of Higher Education*, August 18, 1995, p. A19–A22.

Class 27
Discussion on intellectual property and information security.

Reading assignments:
D. B. Quinn, "The Information Age: Another Giant Step Backward," *The Journal of Academic Librarianship*, (July 1994): 134–135.
James Fallows. "Not yet Net," *Atlantic Monthly* 275 (May 1995): 108–112.

WEEK 10

Class 28
Catch-up. If we are not behind, we can discuss the dark side of the Web and computer technologies. A reading list will be provided for your fun and edification, nothing from the discussion or reading list will be on the exam.

Class 29
Catch-up/review of material.

Class 30
Third exam/final paper due.

© 1995 Rosemary Young. Reprinted with permission.

COURSE SYLLABUS, ASSIGNMENTS, AND EXAMS

In designing a syllabus, try to balance different technologies to give students exposure to a variety of resources. The sample syllabus in Figure 5.1 provides for a three-credit-hour, lower-division, information literacy course. The course is meant to introduce students to information literacy skills at the beginning of their academic careers and places heavy emphasis on evaluative skills.

- Class 1: This first session is for introductions and course overview.
- Classes 2–3: Discussions in these classes help students understand the impact of technology on information and establish the importance of information literacy for success in the working world.
- Classes 4–5: These sessions give students an overview of information sources before delving into specific tools.
- Classes 6–7: Classes give an overview of searching strategies, with emphasis on the transferability of these strategies.
- Classes 8–9: The discussion in class 8 on evaluating sources sets the scene for the first exam.
- Classes 10–14: The students apply the search strategies to a variety of database types.
- Classes 15–17: Criteria for evaluating both the databases searched and the documents retrieved are introduced and applied throughout these class sessions. Students identify primary and secondary sources, explore popular and scholarly literature, familiarize themselves with current and retrospective works as well as concise or in-depth works, and analyze point of view and objectivity. They discuss how to analyze authors' credentials and affiliations. All of the discussions and assignments are meant to set a tone of critical inquiry.
- Class 18: This is the second exam.
- Classes 19–20: These are devoted to government documents. Discussions emphasize the need for free and open access to government information in a democratic society.
- Classes 21–24: Four classes are devoted to searching techniques on the Web, with extensive discussions on evaluation.
- Classes 25–30: The final class sessions concentrate on privacy, security of information, and intellectual property in an electronic age.

The goal of all of these discussions is to convey a sense of the importance of information and the necessity of knowing how to access and evaluate information.

The assignments listed in the syllabus are designed to reinforce the lessons from the classroom. The writing assignment for class 2 is especially revealing. When students are asked to explore their own information-seeking behavior, many are surprised by how limiting their behavior is. The discussions at the following class can be candid and can set the tone for all discussions for the remainder of the classes.

Other assignments require students to apply various criteria they have learned from their readings and classroom discussions: the writing assignment for class 11 has students compare several databases, the assignment for class 12 involves identifying bias and noise, and the writing assignment for class 17 has the student evaluate an article.

A sample test is shown in Figure 5–2. The test is designed to require students to apply the evaluative skills that they have acquired through the class.

In today's world, students must be prepared to access and critically analyze information. The library is the perfect setting for this type of learning. A full-credit course gives librarians the opportunity to stimulate students' interest in these lifelong learning skills.

Figure 5.2   Sample Test for Information Literacy Course

100 points possible

Question 1.
Examine the periodicals in your packet, noting that each is numbered (1, 2, 3, 4). Recalling the criteria you've learned for distinguishing scholarly journals, trade journals, general-interest magazines, and popular magazines, fill in the intent, intended audience, authors credentials, presence of references, and your overall analysis of the type of publications you have in hand. (20 points)

Periodical #1

Title:

Intent

Intended Audience

Authors

References

Overall Classifications

Periodical #2

Title:

Intent

Intended Audience

Authors

References

Overall Classification

Periodical #3

Title:

Intent

Intended Audience

Authors

References

Overall Classification

Periodical #4

Title:

Intent

Intended Audience

Authors

References

Overall Classification

Question 2
Define what is meant by a "refereed journal." (5 points)

Question 3
Why is the "referee" process important to scholarly research journals? (5 points)

Question 4
We have discussed five types of Web pages in class. Please list these five and describe each. (15 points)

Question 5
List the five traditional evaluation criteria for print resources. (10 points)

Question 6
Adapt these five traditional evaluation criteria to Web resources. (10 points)

Question 7
Using the evaluation criteria you have listed in question 6, compare these two Web sites related to AIDS.

Web site #1: www.cdc.gov/nchstp/hiv-aids/stats/exposure.htm

Web site #2: 147.129.1.10/library/lib2/AIDSFACTS.htm
Please list your analysis of each criterion for each site.

After completing this task, tell me which of the two do you think is a reliable resource for research about AIDS? Why? (total of 35 points)

NOTES

1. Deborah Fink, "Information, Technology, and Library Research" in *Conceptual Frameworks for Bibliographic Instruction: Theory into Practice,* ed. Mary Reichel and Mary Ann Ramey, Littleton, Colo.: Libraries Unlimited Incorporated, (1987) pp. 24–35.
2. Larry Hardesty, "Faculty Culture and Bibliographic Instruction: An Exploratory Analysis," *Library Trends* 44 (1995): 339.
3. Eugene Engeldinger, "Frustration Management in a Course-Integrated Bibliographic Instruction Program," *RQ* 32 (fall 1992): 20–24.
4. Fink, "Information, Technology, and Library Research," pp. 26–28.

6 EVALUATION OF INFORMATION LITERACY INSTRUCTION

It is necessary to evaluate information literacy programs to measure the program's effectiveness and to give direction for improvement. The evaluation process must be ongoing, as information literacy programs adapt to meet the users' changing needs. Constructing appropriate evaluation tools and implementing an evaluation plan is a complex undertaking that requires careful thought and planning. There may be multiple goals of an evaluation, such as evaluating the instructional methodology used or measuring student progress.

Many librarians find it difficult to incorporate an evaluation component into their information literacy training. Constructing and implementing an adequate evaluation program is time consuming, and librarians' already excessive workloads may mean they may have too little time and too few resources to conduct appropriate ones. As a result, librarians often rely on informal observations or verbal comments from a few students as an evaluation tool. These types of evaluation tools must be used with caution, however, as they may be slanted by the subjectivity of the observer.

Due to their lack of time and resources, librarians are looking to the library literature to learn how best to focus their efforts. Librarians are also experiencing some outside pressure to develop a systematic approach to assessing their information literacy programs. As Christopher Bober and his colleagues point out: "Growing concern about college and university graduates' ability to think critically and demonstrate problem solving behavior has ushered in the era of accountability in higher education. As libraries are subjected to ever-increasing external scrutiny, the quality of evaluations conducted will have to improve. The need to justify expenditures on user education programs will necessitate a more systematic approach to evaluation."[1]

DETERMINING THE PURPOSE OF EVALUATION

Goals and objectives must be considered carefully before undertaking an evaluation program. Is the purpose of the evaluation program to provide information for self-improvement for the instructor? Or will the evaluation have a broader purpose and be used by administration for making personnel decisions? Is the program evaluation to help make decisions in curriculum development?

There are multiple reasons for evaluating and ways of doing it. The way the information will be used affects what and how information will be collected. Evaluative tools and strategies come and go from favor, and there is no perfect tool for evaluating. Thus, it is important to design an evaluation that meets the instructional needs of the librarian, the course content, and the instructional setting.

If the use of the evaluation is for self-improvement of the instructor, highly detailed information that describes the strengths and weaknesses of the instructor is generally preferred (a *formative evaluation*). If the use is for personnel decisions, then information that measures the overall competence of the instructor is preferred (a *summative evaluation*).[2]

Ideally, librarians want to improve their presentation skills and experiment until they find the best way to present information literacy concepts to their students. This means they need to have the freedom to try out new methods, search examples, or new technologies, and then be open to feedback about the impact of their teaching through evaluations. They need the leeway to explore and occasionally to fail without fear that they will be penalized for experimenting with new techniques.

If the purpose is to improve the teaching skills of the librarian, and ideally this is the case, then formative evaluation as opposed to summative evaluation should be used. Librarians at Arizona State University West make a strong case for formative evaluations:

> The primary function of the evaluation program must be formative rather than summative. In other words, the focus must be on improving the teaching effectiveness of the librarians and the overall effectiveness of the instruction program rather than on assessing the librarians for personnel-related reasons. Summative evaluation should be secondary because the evaluation program must be nonjudgmental and supportive to assure constructive cooperation. The purpose of the program is to reduce the threat inherent in evaluation."[3]

STEPS IN THE INSTRUCTIONAL IMPROVEMENT PROCESS

In order to improve your teaching methods; you must first understand how you teach. This requires an in-depth self-analysis of your teaching style, which follows seven steps.

Step 1. Carefully review your course materials and do self-observation. If you are lucky enough to have videotaping capability in the classroom, use it. The videotapes do not have to be shared with anyone else. A brutally honest tool, the videotape will not try to spare your feelings as a colleague might. It can help you discover annoying habits or show that you slip from active learning techniques into a lecture mode as a class progresses.

Step 2. Collect feedback on how you teach. Gather information from students in your class and from faculty who are team teaching information literacy classes with you. Ask colleagues to attend your presentations and give you feedback. (The tools used to do this are discussed in the next section of this chapter.) The information collected must be highly detailed, diagnostic, and focused on specific course characteristics or teaching behaviors in order to pinpoint the necessary changes for improvement. Enough information must be collected to verify its validity and reliability (this will be dealt with later in this chapter).

Step 3. See what others are doing. Librarians know the importance of keeping current with the literature on teaching methodologies. Many of us not only read professional journals but also subscribe to numerous listservs that enable us to discuss the latest issues with our peers. One of the most important listservs for librarians involved in library instruction is the Bibliographic Instruction Listserv (BI-L) moderated by Martin Raish. Librarians are also attuned to the importance of attending workshops and conferences that help them keep their skills current. Yet another excellent source is visiting a colleague's class. It is very instructive to see how another librarian may be able to capture the interest of the students and maintain that interest throughout the class. You can then use these new examples and techniques in your own classroom.

Step 4. Compare your self-evaluation with the feedback. Compare your understanding of how you teach with the feedback from your students, faculty, and colleagues. Then compare your self-analysis with information gleaned from published information and discussions with colleagues. The comparisons can prove enlightening even to the most experienced teacher and should help you see where change is needed in your course presentation and content.

Step 5. Decide what to change and how to change it. Review your policies and practices in light of your institution's educational goals and objectives. Look at your teaching behaviors in light of your multiple evaluative sources. Then make informed decisions on where changes should be made and use information gleaned from professional development activities to decide how to make the changes.

Step 6. Incorporate the changes into your teaching. We recommend that you make changes gradually and systematically. Changing familiar ways of teaching is difficult, but through gradual change, a small improvement can be implemented and mastered before moving on to the next. Decisions on what to tackle first in this gradual improvement process are up to you.

Step 7. Assess the impact of the changes you made. This is the final step in the instructional improvement process. It requires that you return to the first step of the process and repeat everything discussed in this section. You must evaluate if the changes you made were successful. You must evaluate if your teaching has become more effective. Simply put, the evaluation of instruction is a never-ending process.

EVALUATION INSTRUMENTS

Once you have a clear understanding of the purpose of your evaluation and the steps involved, you are better prepared to develop the evaluation instrument. Although most of your energy will probably go toward evaluating student perceptions and mastery of material, it is also important to plan to get faculty perceptions and to include them in the process. Keeping your goals in mind and how you will be using the information you gather, you are ready to begin.

STUDENT SURVEYS/QUESTIONNAIRES

One of the most popular means of evaluating instruction is the student survey or questionnaire to glean the students' perceptions. Through questionnaires, you can discover if students "liked" the method used to teach the class and if students "think" they learned something from the presentation. This "reaction data" is the most frequently used method to assess the effectiveness of library instruction. Keep in mind that this type of survey or questionnaire cannot give you a definitive picture of what students actually learned, so a total reliance on these attitudinal questionnaires for evaluating library-skills programs may not be in your best interest.

A questionnaire can include open-ended questions, closed-ended questions, or a combination of these. The American Library Association recently published an excellent book containing an outstanding collection of questions and forms for this type of evaluation.[4] The bulk of this book consists of questions you can use to construct your own questionnaire. The questions are grouped by the type of information being sought, such as questions on demographics, the patrons' library background, on presentation and content, and the like. Just remember that a survey instrument constructed only from these questions does not measure student learning, it measures what students think they learned.

Figure 6.1 shows a student questionnaire that we developed to determine students' reaction to an instructional videotape that was designed to teach freshmen how to use the university libraries' OPAC, and to introduce students to several specific search capabilities of the OPAC. You can use it in your setting simply by changing the names of the online systems. The videotape was a new format for teaching freshmen and possibly needed further editing. We had several purposes in mind for the evaluation:

1. We wanted to know students' reaction to being taught via videotape.
2. We wanted to know if the students found the videotape presentation boring or stimulating.
3. We wanted to know if students felt they grasped the specific skills that we wanted to teach through the videotape presentation.

You will see from examining the survey that we limited our questions to information pertinent to our purposes. Because we wanted to know students' reaction to the videotape program, the attitudinal survey was an appropriate evaluation tool to choose.

Figure 6.1   UC Libraries UCLID/OhioLINK Evaluation

Please take a few minutes to fill out this survey to help evaluate the teaching effectiveness of the presentation you just watched. **THIS IS NOT A TEST!!** There are no right or wrong answers. For each question, circle the number from **1 to 5 on the scale** that best represents what YOU think of the video. We appreciate your honest, constructive criticism. When you are finished, please give the survey to your instructor.

	1	2	3	4	5
Did you enjoy the video?	1 No, I hated it	2	3 It was OK	4	5 I liked it
How much information was presented in the video?	1 Not enough	2	3 Right amount	4	5 Too much
How easy was it to understand the information presented in the video?	1 Difficult	2	3 It was OK	4	5 Easy
How interesting was the video?	1 Boring	2	3 It was OK	4	5 Interesting
After seeing the video, do you know what UCLID is?	1 I still don't know	2	3 I understand somewhat	4	5 I fully understand
After seeing the video, do you know what resources are included in OhioLINK?	1 I still don't know	2	3 I understand somewhat	4	5 I fully understand
After seeing the video, how well do you understand the differences between UCLID and OhioLINK?	1 I still don't know	2	3 I understand somewhat	4	5 I fully understand
Do you understand the difference between searching for a person as a *subject* and as an *author*?	1 I still don't know	2	3 I understand somewhat	4	5 I fully understand
Do you understand that an author can also be an organization or an agency?	1 I still don't know	2	3 I understand somewhat	4	5 I fully understand
Do you understand the difference between searching for a journal title and searching for an *article* that has appeared in a journal?	1 I still don't know	2	3 I understand somewhat	4	5 I fully understand
Do you now understand the concept of "Library of Congress subject headings"?	1 I still don't know	2	3 I understand somewhat	4	5 I fully understand
Do you understand the various parts of the UCLID screen?	1 I still don't know	2	3 I understand somewhat	4	5 I fully understand

1 of 2

Figure 6.1 (continued)

Do you know how to find additional UCLID commands?	1 I still don't know	2	3 I understand somewhat	4	5 I fully understand
Do you know how to expand a search from UCLID into OhioLINK?	1 I still don't know	2	3 I understand somewhat	4	5 I fully understand
Do you know how to order a book from an OhioLINK library?	1 I still don't understand	2	3 I understand somewhat	4	5 I fully understand
Do you know how to limit your search to a specific library?	1 I still don't understand	2	3 I understand somewhat	4	5 I fully understand
Do you know how to limit your search to a specific year?	1 I still don't understand	2	3 I understand somewhat	4	5 I fully understand
Do you know what is being searched when you do a keyword search?	1 I still don't understand	2	3 I understand somewhat	4	5 I fully understand
Do you understand the difference between a keyword search and a subject search?	1 I still don't understand	2	3 I understand somewhat	4	5 I fully understand
After seeing the video, do you feel comfortable using UCLID or OhioLINK?	1 I don't feel comfortable at all	2	3 I feel somewhat comfortable	4	5 I am completely comfortable
Do you think that Freshman English classes should continue to be shown this video?	1 Definitely should not	2	3 Don't care either way	4	5 Definitely should
How old are you?	1 Under 20	2 20–21	3 22–25	4 26–30	5 Over 30
How many quarters have you been in college?	1 1–2	2 3–4	3 5–6	4 7–9	5 10 or more
Have you used UCLID or OhioLINK before?	1. Yes		2. No		3. Not sure
What is your gender?		1. Female		2. Male	

2 of 2

STUDENT FOCUS GROUPS

Student focus groups can be an important tool in evaluating library instruction programs (see also Chapter 2). Because focus groups are extremely labor intensive, we recommend prudent use of this method. But they are well worth the effort when looking at a complete overhaul of a program or when evaluating a new format for presentation.

We have utilized student focus groups in conjunction with student surveys and tests when introducing and evaluating the new video format for teaching use of the OPAC to freshmen. Figure 6.2 shows the questions used to guide the focus-group discussions.

Figure 6.2   Questions for Focus Group Evaluating Orientation Video

1.   In general, what did you think of the video?

2.   What do you feel about the quantity of information presented in the video?

3.   How easy was it to understand the information presented in the video?

4.   How interesting was the video?

5.   Do you think freshman classes should continue to be shown this video versus in-person orientations by the library staff?

STUDENT TESTS

The use of tests to determine what has been learned is a common evaluation method in library-skills—and other—programs. This is not useful in giving librarians direct feedback on the effect of teaching instruments or their teaching style, but it will determine if students have mastered basic skills. Figure 6.3 gives an example of a basic library-skills test that can be edited to fit your system. This test was used in conjunction with surveys and focus group discussions (shown in Figures 6.1 and 6.2) to evaluate if students understood basic skills presented in videotape.

There is some controversy surrounding the ability of basic library-skills tests to measure the students' actual learning. Bober and colleagues state that "correct answers can often be given through short term recall. Although students may have mastered basic library skills, such as how to read a call number, they may not have acquired the conceptual knowledge necessary to adequately conduct their own research."[6]

Some institutions use pre-tests and post-tests in information literacy classes to ensure that students are learning something new and are not just using skills they possessed prior to the class. Tiefel has raised some questions, however, as to the validity of pretesting. "A pre-test may serve as an advanced organizer of content or it may be that students simply learn from taking the test."[7]

Figure 6.3   UCLID/OhioLINK Exercise

Name: _____   Instructor: _____

Campus (check) OMI/CAS: _____   RWC: _____   Clermont: _____

The following exercise is based on information presented in the UCLID/OhioLINK videotape shown in class. All questions can be answered by using UCLID, and it is intended that you be at a UCLID terminal when doing this exercise.

1.   What letter command is used to find library information about UCLID and OhioLINK from the UCLID main menu?
    a.   U
    b.   E
    c.   I
    d.   F

2.   Can UCLID and OhioLINK be accessed via dial access and or the Internet?
    a.   Yes, both ways
    b.   No, neither way
    c.   Dial access yes, Internet no
    d.   Internet yes, dial access no

3.   Type in the subject search "computer viruses." How many subject headings appear as a result of your search?
    a.   None
    b.   One
    c.   Two
    d.   Three
    e.   More than three

To check on actual books about computer viruses, you would simply type in the number of the specific subject heading you wished to look under and the list of book titles would appear.

Not all subject searches are as easy. If the words you choose are not the subject heading used by the Library of Congress (which is a list of headings used by UCLID and OhioLINK), you will have to do additional steps. The following questions demonstrate this.

4.   As a subject search, type the phrase "Financial Aid." Your result is:
    a.   A list of books on financial aid
    b.   A list of topics and subtopics on financial aid
    c.   "See" cross references to the term "Student Aid"
    d.   No relevant information to the topic financial aid

Type the command "A" to begin a new subject search.

5. Type in the phrase "Presidential Elections" as a subject search. The result shows that "Your SUBJECT not found, nearby subjects are:" This indicates that:
   a. There are no books listed in UCLID under the subject "Presidential Elections"
   b. "Presidential Elections" is not a valid Library of Congress subject heading.
   c. There is no cross reference to the authorized subject heading used by the Library of Congress.
   d. All of the above
   e. None of the above

6. At the bottom of the screen, results from the unsuccessful search in question 5 is an option "W>Same Search as Word Search." Press the command "W" and do this search. What do you get after using the "W" command?
   a. A list of books, all of which are relevant to the topic
   b. A list of books using the words "presidential" and "elections" somewhere in the record
   c. A list of books, none of which are relevant

7. Find a book on the list of results from the above word search that appears relevant to your topic. What subject is actually used in UCLID for "Presidential Elections"?
   a. Commander in chief—Elections
   b. President—United States—Elections
   c. Executive Branch—United States—Elections
   d. Politics and government—United States—Elections

Scenario: Your instructor has recommended that the class read an article in the November 27, 1997, issue of the journal entitled *Infoworld*. You want to know if the OMI/CAS Library has the title and this specific issue.

8. After you have done a title search and selected the entry, which is *Infoworld*, how do you know it is not a BOOK called *Infoworld*? Hint: Check the information in the bibliographic entry.
   a. There is a "frequency" statement that shows issues per year.
   b. There is a "publ history" statement that shows volume and issue numbers.
   c. The subject headings listed have "periodicals" as a subdivision.
   d. All of the above in this case.
   e. None of the above in this case.

9. Two library locations show on the first screen. What command do you give to see more libraries that own this title?
   a. M
   b. B
   c. C
   d. P
   e. V

10. Does the OMI/CAS Library own this title, and have they checked in the issue you want? Hint: For the second part of this question, press the NUMBER of the record for which you wish to see more details.
    a. Yes, they own the title, but do not have the issue.
    b. No, they don't own the title.
    c. Yes, they have both the title and the specific issue.

STUDENT OUTCOMES ASSESSMENT PROCESS

One of the leading movements in education in recent years is out-come-based education, which concentrates on the learner. An essential part of outcome-based education is the development of assessments that reflect goals, requiring critical thinking or the ability to solve complex problems. Students have to synthesize knowledge and use it appropriately, not just regurgitate facts on a test.

The distinction between an assessment and a test is not merely semantic. "An assessment is a comprehensive, multifaceted analysis of performance; it must be judgment-based and personal. It involves the use of a variety of techniques, has a primary reliance on observations (of performance), and involves an integration of (diverse) information in a summary judgment. As distinct from 'psychometric measurement' (or 'testing'), assessment is a form of clinical analysis and prediction of performance. An education test, by contrast, is an 'instrument,' a measuring device."[8]

Principles for Assessing Student Outcomes

Student-outcome assessment is used by many educational accrediting organizations to evaluate teaching effectiveness in academic institutions. There are four principles underlying the process:

1. The college as a whole, as well as each individual department, must have clearly articulated mission statements that define the academic goals upon which all assessment is based.
2. Each area to be assessed must have quantifiable methods to measure the intended outcome.
3. The results from these measures are analyzed and changes are implemented to improve student performance.
4. This assessment process is ongoing and cyclical; new student outcomes are developed and measured over time.

STEPS FOR ASSESSING STUDENT OUTCOMES

Step 1. Identify the specific academic goal upon which to base the student outcomes assessment. For example, the mission statement (unpublished) of the University of Cincinnati Raymond Walters College (RWC) Library sets forth four academic commitments:

(1) We will support the educational and research needs of the RWC college community.
(2) We will provide access to information and promote information literacy.
(3) We will seek input from faculty, staff, and students to help us improve our services and resources.

(4) We will be leaders in professional and community services opportunities.

The specific mission goal for commitment is: "To teach the college community how to locate, evaluate, and effectively use information." Therefore, this mission goal is the basis for assessing the information literacy program of the RWC Library.

Step 2. Develop "statements of intended student outcomes" that describe what the students will know, think, or do upon completing information literacy instruction. An example of an outcome statement is: "Students will be taught how to locate, evaluate, and effectively use information." It is important to note that the emphasis of this assessment technique is upon what the students will learn, and therefore outcome statements must reflect this. A realistic range of outcome statements to develop is at least three but no more than five. As will be described below, there must be at least one measure for each outcome. Obviously, the more outcomes you have, the more time you will spend collecting and analyzing the data for each measure. From the conceptual perspective, one of the goals of this assessment process is to ascertain the overall understanding by students of the information literacy concepts, not each individual course objective. The measures will identify specific areas to focus upon for improvement or change.

To demonstrate the effectiveness of each outcome, you must adopt quantifiable measures such as student and faculty surveys, analysis of library research assignments, and national standards such as those of the Association for College and Research Libraries. Therefore, a measure to evaluate students' understanding of information literacy concepts could be: "Eighty percent of the students responding in a library-instruction survey will say they understand how to find information using print and electronic resources. The evaluation survey will be administered to all students attending instruction sessions." Another measure might be: "Upon reviewing the Freshman English Composition I research paper assignment, 70 percent of the students will have selected appropriate subject headings for their topics." When you initially develop these measures, you may be unsure what percentages or levels are appropriate. Since the purpose of using measures is to establish an acceptable baseline upon which to improve, you will need to consider a number of factors—such as the curriculum (integrated, for-credit, one-time lecture), hands-on computer training, characteristics of the student body, when the instruction is provided (freshman orientation, senior research project), and so forth.

Step 3. Analyze the data you have gathered and use those data to make any necessary changes. Not only is it important to measure how successful you are in achieving the outcomes you established, it is also essential that you evaluate the data and use the results to make changes, such as the course content or the method you use to teach. If, for example, 85 percent of the students you surveyed indicated that they understood how to use print resources, but only 60 percent indicated that they were confident of how to search the electronic resources, then you would need to improve this portion of your program. It could mean increasing the time students experience hands-on instruction, or changing the assignments to emphasize the use of specific electronic resources.

Figure 6.4 and 6.5 illustrate the student-outcome assessment process. The Raymond Walters College Academic Assessment Committee developed this particular format.

Figure 6.4 Assessment Record: Expanded Statement of Institutional Purpose

MISSION:
The Raymond Walters College Library stands by four commitments as an academic department of the college:
(1)   We will support the educational and research needs of the RWC College community.
(2)   We will provide access to information and promote information literacy.
(3)   We will seek input from faculty, staff, and students to help us improve our services and resources.
(4)   We will be leaders in professional and community service opportunities.

GOAL(S):

1.   To teach the college community how to locate, evaluate, and effectively use information.

INTENDED UNIT OUTCOMES

1.   Students will be taught how to locate information.

2.   Students will be taught how to effectively use information.

3.   Students will be taught how to evaluate information.

4.

5.

Figure 6.5   Assessment Record: Intended Unit Outcomes

1. **First outcome:**
   Students will be taught how to locate information.

Summary of <u>first measure,</u> results and uses:

1a. **Measure of Assessment & Criteria for Success:**
   Seventy percent of the students will respond in a library survey that they understand how to find information using print and electronic resources. The evaluation will be administered during all instruction sessions.

1a. **Assessment Results:**
   Eighty-three percent of the students responded that they understood how to use print resources; 63 percent responded that they understood how to use electronic resources. Although most of the lectures provided time for hands-on computer exercises, at least 25 percent did not. In addition, the amount of hands-on time was only fifteen to twenty minutes per session, which may have not been enough time for some students who were not familiar with computers.

1a. **Use of Results:**
   The Instruction Librarian met with the English department for which most of the instructions are offered and proposed the idea of offering additional lab time outside of the classroom lectures for students to gain additional hands-on training. Students will receive extra credit for attending these labs. The English department faculty approved the proposal, which will be implemented Fall Quarter, 1998.

FACULTY QUESTIONNAIRES/INTERVIEWS/FOCUS GROUPS

The teaching faculty should be involved in evaluation of information literacy classes. Figure 3.1 provides a sample questionnaire for a faculty member whose class attends a library-skills session. This questionnaire helps determine the faculty member's reaction to the class content, supporting materials, and the librarian's presentation skills.

It is useful to interview faculty members who team-teach classes with you, or who attend the library-skills sessions with their students. This type of interaction will give you more in-depth answers to questions on how to improve future classes than a written questionnaire. The one-on-one interaction of an interview will also help you establish a strong working relationship with your teaching faculty.

When large groups of faculty are involved in a specific information literacy program, such as a library program for Freshman English, a focus group may be a valuable evaluation tool. Just as philosophies and approaches to teaching Freshman English are as numerous as the instructors, so will be the variety of their opinions on integrating information literacy programs into their classes. By encouraging instructors to air their opinions in a focus-group setting, not only will you be gathering important information for evaluating your information literacy program, but you also will be providing a neutral setting for a diverse faculty to express their perceptions of students' information needs.

THE IMPORTANCE OF USING A VARIETY OF EVALUATIVE METHODS

Be sure to use an assortment of these methods to evaluate your instruction. Don't rely strictly on student questionnaires that immediately follow the presentation for feedback. At Indiana University South Bend, Rosanne Cordell reports that "immediately after each session, students are given a short 'feedback' form to fill out. This gives us information about how well received the session was. Some librarians send more detailed questionnaires for students to fill out after their research project is completed, for a different view. Faculty are also given feedback forms which ask more direct questions."[9]

As already mentioned, we used a combination of student surveys, student focus groups, and student tests to evaluate the introduction of a video for teaching Freshman English students the use of the OPAC, which proved useful in developing the list of required revisions to the video. Formal input from faculty involved in Freshman English classes was overlooked, however, and would have provided valuable information as well.

TECHNICAL QUALITY OF EVALUATION INSTRUMENTS

Evaluation instruments must be both reliable and valid. Reliability occurs when the instruments provide information that is free from biases due to sampling of students, courses, and time of administration. They are reliable if: there is agreement among students within a class in rating the instructor and course; there is consistency to students' ratings of the same instructor at different times; and the same instructor teaching different sections of the same course receives similar ratings from each section. "In general five or more courses of at least fifteen students are needed for a reliable assessment."[10]

Validity indicates that the evaluation tool measures what it is intended to measure. Validity takes into account two factors:

1. To what extent do factors not under the control of the instructor bias student ratings?
2. Do student ratings correlate with other measures?

When considering these factors you may find that students give low ratings to some classes regardless of the instructor. For example, a course in electronic resources that must be held in a classroom that does not have student computer workstations may consistently receive lower ratings than the same class given by the same instructor in a classroom that has student workstations. This demonstrates that the evaluation tool is not actually measuring the instructor's ability to teach but rather students' dissatisfaction with the facility. There are numerous factors that could influence students' ratings, such as class size, the classroom, availability of resources, timing of the class, negative wording of the evaluation tool, and the like. Therefore, evaluation tools must be carefully constructed and be very specific to be valid.

SUMMARY

Obtaining feedback for information literacy programs does not automatically insure teaching skills and course content will improve. The information gathered must be interpreted and applied by the librarian. Though evaluation is a time-consuming task, the results are worth the effort. Librarians must systematically approach the process of implementing changes in how they teach. And above all, librarians need to view the process as an ongoing one.

NOTES

1. Christopher Bober, Sonia Poulin, and Luigina Vileno, "Evaluating Library Instruction in Academic Libraries," *The Reference Librarian*, no. 51–52 (1995): 53–71.
2. Larry A. Braskamp, Dale C. Brandenburg, and John C. Ory, *Evaluating Teaching Effectiveness: A Practical Guide* (Beverly Hills: Sage Press, 1984), p. 31.
3. Dennis Isbell, "A Formative, Collegial Approach to Evaluating Course-Integrated Instruction at Arizona State University West," *Research Strategies* 12 (winter 1994): 24–32.
4. Diane Shonrock, *Evaluating Library Instruction* (Chicago: American Library Association, 1996).
5. D. W. Stewart and P. N. Sharndasarri, *Focus Groups: Theory and Practice* (Newbury Park, CA: Sage, 1990), p. 414.
6. Bober, Poulin, and Vileno, "Evaluating Library Instruction," p. 59.
7. Virginia Tiefel, "Evaluating a Library User Education Program, a Decade of Experience," *College and Research Libraries* 50 (March 1989): 249–259.
8. Grant P. Wiggins, *Assessing Student Performance: Exploring the Purpose and Limits of Testing* (San Francisco: Jossey-Bass, 1993), p. 12–13.
9. Rosanne Cordell, Bibliographic Instruction Listserv, posted May 27, 1997.
10. Helen Rippier Wheeler, *The Bibliographic Instruction Handbook* (Metuchen, NJ: Scarecrow Press, 1988), p. 44.

7 USING INSTRUCTIONAL TECHNOLOGIES TO ENHANCE INFORMATION LITERACY INSTRUCTION

An integral part of the teaching process is the effective use of instructional technologies to enhance the content of the classroom presentation and course assignments. Gone are the days of the "talking head" lecture with the overhead transparency sheets. The availability and variety of software programs, such as PowerPoint and HTML editors for Web design, make it possible for anyone to produce effective presentations and instructional materials. Many of these software packages are relatively inexpensive and can operate on standard microcomputers (those with Pentium chips or 486s with a reasonable amount of memory) that most people have in their office. The major investment on your part will be the time to learn these technologies. In most cases you will also need to have a basic understanding and working knowledge of Windows commands and features.

The purpose of this chapter is to provide an introduction to key design considerations in developing tools using instructional technologies. Obviously, there are numerous texts on designing Web sites and producing mulitmedia and video products. However, before you embark on such endeavors, you need to understand several production and design principles. This chapter reviews the overall planning and production process for designing and creating presentations. It focuses upon three types of instructional technologies that most college libraries have access to: video, presentation software, and Web tutorials.

PLANNING AND PRODUCTION PROCESS

Regardless of the type of instructional technology that you will be using, there is a planning and production process that you will need to undertake to design a product that meets your teaching objectives. The following outline of a production process was designed by H. Michael Sanders, Director of the Raymond Walters College Media Services Center.[1] Although this process is geared toward major multimedia productions, these planning principles are applicable to smaller projects.

As you set up your own process, document how you designed your tool, what technical decisions you made, and what source material you used, because you will need this information for future revisions.

PROJECT DEVELOPMENT

Your first step is to define clearly and precisely what your educational goals are and how this instructional tool will enhance the learning process. It is particularly important to identify your target audience. Although this point may seem obvious, it is not always as easy as you may think. For example, if your academic institution enrolls a significant number of "nontraditional" students (such as students working full-time jobs, older adult students), then it can be especially challenging to find an approach that captures their interest in a meaningful way. Another consideration is the type of instructional technology that would be best suited to convey your content. If you are uncertain what technology to use, consult media specialists. Many academic institutions have media production departments with staff whose expertise include instructional design.

Seven steps in project design:

Step 1. Project idea

Step 2. Project goal development: Educational outcomes

Step 3. Project needs assessment:
- How will this instructional tool enhance the students' learning process?
- How will this tool fit into your overall information literacy instruction program?

Step 4. Analysis:
- Specific objectives: How will the instructional goals be accomplished?
- Target audience identification: Be very specific about the intended audience. If you are not, then your presentation may become too general and lack meaningful content.

Step 5. Production context:
- Production medium: Web, video, interactive CD, etc.
- Delivery platform: hardware
- Authoring platform: software

Step 6. Usage/Delivery context: Classroom lecture, individual training module

Step 7. Project management
- Project time line
- Project budget development
- Approval cycle and sign-offs: Who must review the product and give final approval for the finished product?
- Roles and responsibilities of the production team and client
- Resources and personnel

PREPRODUCTION (DESIGN)

Once you have decided upon your project goals and the technology, you need to determine the content. You should spend a considerable amount of time on planning your content, because this is what "fleshes out" your outline of key instructional concepts to become the actual script of the tutorial. You also need to identify how this script will be presented through graphics, links to Web sites, what types of fonts and colors to use, and so forth.

Six preproduction steps

1. Content research:
   - Material collection: graphics, sound clips, photographs, etc.
   - Concept generation: brainstorming

2. Project content outline: Subject content of the presentation

3. Project treatment (synopsis): How will the information be presented? (Graphics or sound, what font, transitions from one part of the presentation to the next, etc.)

4. Project storyboard: The storyboard is a step-by-step overview of the narrative content, visuals, audio, and technical aspects (such as transitions, special effects). Designers will often use 3 x 5 index cards that include the subject content, graphics, and technical details for each slide/video frame/Web page. Storyboarding also addresses two critical components in the design process: sequencing the slides/video frames/Web pages in a logical order; and continuity of the presentation.

5. Project navigation map: A detailed flow chart of how all the project elements fit together and in what sequence

6. Project management:
   - Production breakdown
   - Production schedule
   - Production budget

PRODUCTION

Now you are ready to begin the actual production of your instructional tool (or turn it over to the media production experts). The following steps pertain primarily to major multimedia productions and are included for your information, should you become involved in such a project. If you are producing your project using presentation software or creating a Web site, then the first and last steps (art and graphics, authoring) are the most relevant.

Four Production Steps

1. Production: Art and graphics
   - Graphic look and interface design
   - Content graphics
   - Animation

2. Production: Location and studio
   - Audio production
   - Photo production
   - Video production

3. Production: Digital post
   - Digitize analog sources
   - Audio and music editing
   - Image editing and manipulation
   - Video editing

4. Production: Authoring (programming)
   - Input of content
   - Combination of elements
   - Transitions and effects
   - Testing functionality

POSTPRODUCTION

Once you have completed production, you must spend time testing your project. Ask colleagues who were not involved in the design and production process to review your presentation/tutorial to test both the content and the technical components for errors or problems. You might want also to include several students to participate in this testing and evaluation phase.

The Five Final Steps in the Production Process

1. Testing and evaluation

2. Validation and revision: Correct any problems discovered during the testing phase
3. Documentation
4. Duplication: CD-ROM, video, laser videodisc, floppy disc, slides, etc.
5. Packaging and distribution

VIDEO PROGRAMS

A well-produced videotape can be an effective way to present general principles about library research and information literacy such as describing the organization of the literature, defining the topic of the research paper and selecting appropriate subject headings, and evaluating resources. A creative presentation using sound, images, and action can illustrate key concepts in such a way that a straightforward lecture never could. The video can be used in a variety of circumstances: to complement the classroom lecture; to circulate to students who missed the lecture; to place on reserve as supplementary course materials.

There are two major drawbacks in designing and producing a videotape. First, the costs are very high because of the staff expertise and production process itself. Unlike designing a Web tutorial, which you can do at your desk, creating a video program requires a well-equipped production studio and staff trained in video production. The standard cost for video programs is $1,000 per minute of tape. If your institution has the production capabilities and staff expertise, you may be able to negotiate lower costs by contributing your time in conducting the content research and writing the script. By way of illustration, we created a forty-minute videotape on search techniques for the university OPAC for Freshman English. Even with the cost breaks of contributing our time, the price tag to produce this video was $25,000.

The second drawback is the difficulty in revising the content. Although it is possible to make a few minor revisions, it is difficult to make any major changes unless you are willing to spend a considerable amount of money. Therefore, you should not produce a video on topics that change constantly, such as search techniques for specific databases or Internet search engines.

PRESENTATION SOFTWARE

Presentation software programs, such as PowerPoint or Harvard Graphics, give you with the capability to integrate text and graphics into a program that will enhance the content of your classroom lecture. For example, you can download screens from your OPAC and "jazz" them up with color, additional graphics, and explanatory text to highlight a specific point. Many of these packages include design templates or content outlines that you can adapt to create an aesthetically pleasing and effective presentation—without having to obtain a degree in graphic design! Considerable progress has been made in designing presentation packages that have Internet and HTML capabilities, making it possible to publish your presentation on the Web.

There are a number of presentation packages to choose from that range in price from $100 to $400 or more. Many of these packages are already included in desktop office suites such as MicroSoft Office and Lotus Smart Suite. Before selecting a package that best meets your needs, you must address several issues:

1. What type of information do you want to demonstrate? Will the focus of the presentations be upon concepts or skills or a combination?
2. How will you use this presentation to enhance your presentation? Will you need a software package that includes a wide range of graphics and multimedia capabilities because of the content of your presentation?
3. How much time are you willing to invest in learning how to use the software?

A presentation software–based lecture can effectively instruct students on the essential concepts of defining their research topic and evaluating resources. You can emphasize specific points by projecting onto the screen the key words or phrases of these points. Some packages include special effects that enable you to display a slide line-by-line, highlighting the current line and dimming the previous lines so you can pace your presentation and focus students on what you are currently discussing, rather than reading ahead and missing some of your lecture.

As stated earlier, you can use presentation software to capture screens from your OPAC or research databases and create simulated searches, to highlight certain features of the database to illustrate search strategies and functions. You can use the presentation-based program in tandem with live demonstrations, which can be extremely effective in emphasizing key concepts as you move back and forth between the slides and online database. Creating presentation-software programs for your OPAC and other databases can serve as a back-up when your network goes down, or when you are in a classroom that does not have a network connection.

DESIGN RECOMMENDATIONS

As you design your presentation-software program, remember one simple guideline: keep it simple! These packages provide an incredible array of graphics, colors, fonts, and special effects that make it very easy to go overboard. Remember that these features are to enhance, not obscure your content. Following are a number of design suggestions that can help.[2]

Text

- Be consistent in using type fonts and sizes, uppercase text, margins, borders, and color.
- Keep the text brief, using short phrases or keywords.
- Use bullets.
- List one concept per slide.
- Use type fonts that are easy to read.
- Limit the number of different fonts.

Graphics

- Use images that add emphasis but do not overshadow the text.
- Use recurring images that appear in the same place on every slide.
- Remember copyright issues if you incorporate scanned visuals, video clips, or sound.

Colors

- Do not use more than four different colors per slide.
- Select colors that contrast in luminance and shade.
- Be careful in using background patterns, because they may interfere with the text.
- Test the colors you selected on the hardware you will be using, such as the LCD panel, because they may appear differently when projected onto the screen.

WEB TUTORIALS

The Web offers powerful technology that makes it possible to create interactive multimedia tutorials that can be used for course assignments or self-paced learning modules. Unlike the computer-based instruction programs that were popular a number of years ago, the Web is an integrated teaching tool, because students are using the actual resource itself to learn as well as to conduct their research. If you plan to incorporate a Web tutorial in your instruction program, make sure the students who will be using these tutorials know how to use Web browsers; otherwise, all of your efforts will be in vain.

Many of the design guidelines concerning content, text, and graphics discussed in the production and planning process and presentation-software sections are relevant to Web tutorials: look into HTML editors that make the design and coding relatively easy; determine your target audience carefully; use graphics sparingly; avoid "information overkill mode" of pages that are dense with text that students will not read. Other factors to keep in mind, though, are keeping the tutorial to a reasonable time frame and how the Web can enhance the information you are presenting. Do not simply convert your print handouts or the script from a "live" presentation into a Web-based tutorial. Although it is easy to convert these materials into HTML, it is much harder to make them work like (or better than) your live presentation.

Take advantage of the interactivity that the Web environment offers. For a tutorial on a database that can be accessed online, include links to the database itself so that the student can make a "trial run." The Web is also a great tool to provide feedback, such as through assignments or evaluations that the student completes online and e-mails to you and the faculty member.

You will find many interesting examples of Web-based tutorials on the Internet from which you can get some ideas on how to design your own tutorial. Links to these tutorials can be accessed at a number of Web sites such as that of the University of California (Berkeley) Library Web (www.lib.berkeley.edu/TeachingLib/BIResources/html). You might consider subscribing to electronic discussion groups that focus upon designing Web sites and providing Internet training. Two such discussion groups are:

web4lib@library.berkeley.edu
nettrain@ubvm.cc.buffalo.edu

One word of caution: copyright! Remember, these are copyrighted materials. You should not simply lift the source code from these tutorials and insert your text, because that constitutes copyright infringement. Be sure to contact the list owner for permission to use or copy materials.

SAMPLE OF A WEB-BASED TUTORIAL

Figures 7.1 through 7.4 show the pages from the Raymond Walters College Library Web tutorial, "Searching for Information: The Steps (SFITS)." The student begins at the SFITS page shown in Figure 7.1, which briefly explains how to decide how complex a given topic is. Based on a comparison of the student's topic with the sample topics, the student chooses a strategy to follow based on the topic's level of specificity: a broad topic, a narrow topic, or a factual question.

Once the student has clicked on the topic type, a page showing the strategy for the topic appears (see Figure 7.2). The page lists between six and eight electronic or print sources or source categories. The student is guided to follow the strategy by choosing the sources in the order given. The student may also return to the SFITS page to select another strategy.

After choosing a source, a page appears that briefly describes the source. If it is an electronic source, the page has a direct link to the source and a link to either a tutorial or guide screen for the source (see Figure 7.3). For print sources, a page that explains the source appears and refers the student to other documentation (either online or print) or to a librarian for further assistance.

For the electronic sources the lower part of the frame displays the source connection, and the upper frame has a link back to the strategy page. At any time, the student can quickly return to the strategy page from either electronic or print sources to choose another source from the list or decide that this strategy is not working and go to the Refining Your Search page (see Figure 7.4). This page lists tips for improving the search. It may lead the user to begin the search process over from the SFITS page or to abandon the search from the page and return to the main Raymond Walters College Library Home Page.

The basic idea behind SFITS is to direct the student through the maze of sources available. The guided-search interface described above allows the student to follow selected search strategies to access the information needed. SFITS can be used as a tutorial to teach good search strategies and the use of selected sources. It can also serve as a stand-alone searching aid for students connecting to the library's electronic resources from remote sites. The URL for the complete tutorial is:

www.rwc.uc.edu/library/library/sfitsweb/sfits.htm

Figure 7.1

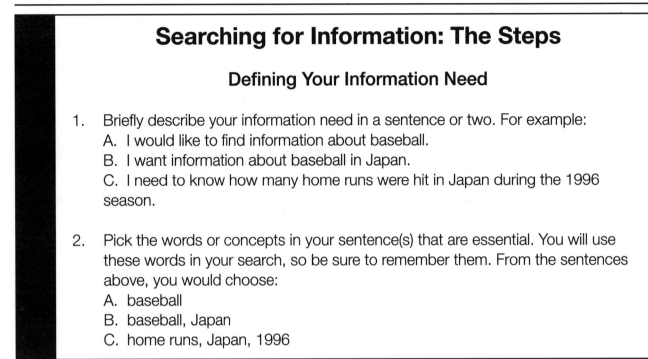

Searching for Information: The Steps

Defining Your Information Need

1. Briefly describe your information need in a sentence or two. For example:
   A. I would like to find information about baseball.
   B. I want information about baseball in Japan.
   C. I need to know how many home runs were hit in Japan during the 1996 season.

2. Pick the words or concepts in your sentence(s) that are essential. You will use these words in your search, so be sure to remember them. From the sentences above, you would choose:
   A. baseball
   B. baseball, Japan
   C. home runs, Japan, 1996

Figure 7.2

Broad Topic Search Strategy

To find information on your broad topic, follow the strategy below. Click on the name of the source you would like to try. We recommend using the sources in the order given below.

1. <u>General encyclopedias</u>
2. <u>Britannica Online</u>
3. <u>UCLID</u>
4. <u>Infotrac Searchbank</u> and/or <u>Periodical Abstracts</u>
5. <u>SIRS Researcher</u>
6. <u>Search the Internet</u>

If you have not found the information you needed or your search is otherwise unsuccessful after using this strategy, look at the <u>Refining Your Search</u> page for assistance.

Figure 7.3

UCLID

UCLID is the online library catalog for all of the libraries within the University of Cincinnati. All books, audiovisual materials, and periodicals which are owned by the libraries are listed in this source. Click on the UCLID to connect to the source. Click on the Tutorial to learn more about using UCLID.

You may also return to the Broad Topic Search Strategy to choose another source.

Figure 7.4

Refining Your Search

If your search was not successful, consider changing your approach. This may require you to repeat some of the steps you've already taken. The suggestions below may be useful:

○ You may need to change your information need sentence(s). Consider making your topic more **narrow** (if you find too many sources) or perhaps more **broad** (if you find too few). You can return to the <u>Searching for Information: The Steps</u> page to review this part of the process.

○ You may need to use other search words or concepts. Think of related words to use in new searches (synonyms, related terms, broader or narrower concepts). For example, if your search terms were **history**, **baseball**, and **Japan**, you could use the following terms instead of, or along with, your original search terms.

NOTES

1. H. Michael Sanders, "Multimedia Planning and Development: An Overview of the Process." Raymond Walters College Media Services Center, University of Cincinnati, 1995. (In-house publication for course on multimedia production)
2. Dennis Strasser. "Tips for Good Electronic Presentations," *ONLINE Magazine* 20 (1) (January/February 1996): 78–81.

8 KEEPING ORGANIZED AND ON TRACK

There are a lot of administrative details, arrangements, and records you will need to organize and manage in support of your instructional programs. This chapter offers a number of suggestions on developing policies; scheduling; designing and teaching in an electronic classroom; and managing your instructional materials.

LIBRARY INSTRUCTION POLICY STATEMENT

It is essential that you develop a policy statement that clearly defines what type of instructional services you will offer and delineates the responsibilities for you and the faculty member (see Figure 8–1 for a sample). Some of the issues to address when drafting your policy statement are:

- what type of instruction modules you will provide
- how this instruction will be provided (such as hands-on practice, classroom demonstrations, tours)
- scheduling procedures (including how much advanced notice is required, handling scheduling conflicts)
- information that faculty should provide for content development (for example, copies of the syllabus or course assignments)
- responsibilities on arranging for the equipment and/or scheduling the electronic classroom
- responsibility of the librarian and faculty member in developing the content and in participating in the instructional process for course-integrated instruction
- responsibility of the librarian and faculty member in creating and grading the library-research assignment for course integrated instruction.

Once you have drafted your instruction policy, you need to disseminate it to the faculty through a variety of channels, such as in your institution's faculty handbook, on the library's (and college's) Web page, and in orientation packets for new faculty. If you have a library committee, you might want them to review your policy; getting their "stamp of approval" can reinforce to the faculty the importance of your instructional program.

Figure 8.1   Guidelines for Arranging a Library Instruction Session

The Library faculty encourage all instructors to schedule library-instruction sessions for their classes. Popular instruction topics include finding books and journal articles, searching the Internet, and critically evaluating information. We can also work with you to design specialized instruction sessions that meet the specific needs of your students.

When scheduling instruction, please note the following:

1. Schedule at least one week in advance. We need at least a week to adequately prepare an effective instruction session. Requests made without the minimum week's notice will not be honored.

2. Schedule customized sessions a minimum of two weeks in advance. Please take into consideration the amount of preparation time we need to create the content and handouts for specialized topics.

3. Requests are scheduled on a first-come, first-served basis. Please include an alternate date on the request form in case of conflict.

4. Please provide us with a copy of the student assignment and a course syllabus along with your request. Knowing what you expect from your students helps us to prepare a more effective instruction session.

5. We will contact you to discuss what information sources and skills you would like your students to know. Please let us know what your goals and expectations are for the session.

6. Your presence during our session sends the message to your students that library instruction is important.

7. Hands-on instruction sessions can be arranged contingent upon the availability of a computer lab. (Scheduling early helps!) We will schedule the lab and verify the location with you.

8. Instruction sessions with some hands-on instruction can be held in the library provided the class is fewer than twelve students.

9. We will schedule the equipment needed for the presentation.

10. You can help us make our library instruction sessions a success! Here are some ways you can participate:

    A. Library instruction is most effective when students will need to use it for a specific assignment. We will be happy to work with you to create an ideal library research assignment, or to discuss the appropriateness of an existing assignment. Please ask!

B. Schedule the instruction session close to the due date of the assignment, allowing students enough time to complete it. In general, the instruction session is most effective three weeks before the due date of the assignment.

C. Discuss the assignment with the students before the day of the instruction session. Make sure they understand your requirements. Also let them know a librarian will be explaining the resources and search strategies they will need to complete the assignment successfully.

D. We encourage you to ask us a question or two during our presentation. Your participation helps clarify and reinforce important aspects of our instruction.

E. We also invite you to comment on the relevancy of the instruction to the students' coursework during the session. (For example, "You'll need to know this to complete your next assignment.") One ingenious faculty member tells students they will earn extra credit by defining a designated term from the instruction session on their final exams.

F. As students are progressing on their assignments, encourage them to ask a librarian if they need assistance with information resources or searching techniques.

SCHEDULING

The following suggestions should make the scheduling of course-integrated and nonintegrated sessions efficient and reduce the problems of double booking or misunderstandings with faculty:

- Delegate scheduling to one person, if more than one librarian shares the responsibility for providing instruction.
- Maintain an up-to-date calendar that other staff can easily access when the scheduling coordinator is unavailable.
- Verify in writing (or electronically) with the faculty member the content, date, place, and time.

Figure 8.2 contains a sample form for faculty to use in scheduling a session. Figure 8.3s form is for the library's use in keeping track of requests.

Figure 8.2 Faculty Request Form for Library Instruction

1. Name_____   2. Date _____

3. Department _____ _____   4. Course name _____

5. What date and time would you like us to come to your class?

1st Choice

	Date	Time
section 1		
section 2		
section 3		
section 4		

2nd Choice

	Date	Time
section 1		
section 2		
section 3		
section 4		

6. Where would you prefer to have the library instruction?

    _____ Computer lab

    _____ Your classroom: Room # sess. 1 _____ sess. 2 _____ sess. 3 _____ sess. 4 _____

    _____ Library (not recommended for groups larger than 12 students)

7. What would you like your students to learn from this library instruction session?

    _____

    _____

8. Should the library instruction be geared toward a specific assignment your students will be completing? If so, please describe the assignment. (It is very helpful to us if you provide us with any handouts you give to students explaining the assignment.)

    _____

    _____

9. How many students are in your class? (approximately)_____

10. Phone number(s) where you can be reached _____

A library faculty member will contact you to discuss the content of the instruction session and to confirm the date and time. We will make the necessary arrangements such as equipment and computer lab scheduling.

Thank you for helping us promote library and information literacy skills!

Figure 8.3 Library Instruction Scheduling Form: For Library Use Only

Library contact's initials _____   Date request received _____

Instructor's name _____   Course title _____

	day & date	time	location	librarian
session 1				
session 2				
session 3				
session 4				

Reservations

    Equipment: Date requested _____   Date confirmed _____

    Computer Lab: Room #_____   Date of lab request _____   Date confirmed _____

Handouts: _____ # of copies needed

Please specifiy which handout(s) you'll be using:

_____

_____

Any special instructions?

_____

_____

Follow-up: _____ # of students in attendance

Comments

_____

_____

THE PHYSICAL TEACHING ENVIRONMENT

An essential component in your instructional program is the physical environment in which you teach. The availability of electronic classrooms and the status of the network infrastructure within your institution will determine your ability to provide the level of hands-on instruction that you and your faculty deem necessary. If you do not have an electronic classroom that is managed by your library, then you should consider using portable equipment (such as a laptop and LCD overhead projector) for classroom presentations and demonstrations when you are not able to schedule one of the college electronic classrooms. In circumstances such as this, you may wish to offer a "hands-on practice clinic" shortly after your lecture (within two to three days) by scheduling open times for students to stop by the library and spend some time on the computer under your guidance.

THE ELECTRONIC CLASSROOM

The ideal situation (with a few caveats) is to design and manage an electronic classroom within your library.

Word of caution about managing electronic classrooms

There are advantages to designing and managing your own electronic classroom: (1) you determine the design and the equipment that meets your instructional program needs; (2) you have control over the availability and use of the classroom. However, there are two significant challenges to consider before moving ahead with this endeavor: funding and staffing. The initial outlay for an electronic classroom is very expensive. Even more important is ongoing funding to maintain and upgrade the hardware and software; otherwise, your classroom will quickly become obsolete. Therefore, you must determine the level of commitment from your administration to this project. Grants may help initially to establish the classroom or purchase special equipment, but do not rely upon this type of funding for routine support. You must also carefully examine the staffing and subsequent technical skills required to manage the classroom: the amount of time to maintain the hardware, install software, regularly scan the hard drives for unauthorized files, and prepare the room for instruction. Ask yourself how these responsibilities will be delegated and what type of staff training will be necessary. Once you have satisfactorily dealt with all these issues, you can move on to actually setting up your space.

There are no simple formulas or standardized blueprints to use, because each library has a unique set of circumstances regarding curricular needs, budget, space, staffing, and network infrastructure. The first step in the design process is to assess the instructional goals of your program and how this electronic classroom will support these goals. Next, you will need to carefully examine the technical and administrative management issues of the classroom, such as installing and maintaining the equipment, staffing, and ongoing funding. Once these decisions are addressed, you are ready to select the equipment and furnishings and to design the physical layout of the classroom.[1]

Step 1. Assess Instructional Goals

- Define types of instruction and how much hands-on training is required:
    - course-integrated instruction with specific library-research assignments
    - nonintegrated classroom lecture or stand-alone presentations
    - credit courses requiring lecture and hands-on, covering a variety of formats
    - average class size
    - learning methods (e.g., collaborative, which would require workstations that can accommodate small groups)

Step 2. Address Technical and Administrative Issues

- Define how the classroom will be technically managed and by whom:
    - installation and maintenance of hardware and software
    - technical expertise of the library staff to maintain the classroom
    - the technical expertise within the college to assist with maintenance and troubleshooting
    - how this classroom will interface with the college network
    - policies on scheduling, adding software, availability for other uses
    - policies and procedures on maintaining security
- Determine the platforms and multimedia requirements:
    - single or multiple platforms (e.g., IBM-PC compatible or Apple)
    - multimedia software to handle video and sound
    - interface with CD-ROM drives

Step 3. Select Equipment and Furnishings

- Instructor workstation:
    - must be configured to connect to a projection system for lecture and demonstration purposes
    - consider installing software that can control the individual workstations to prevent students from playing instead of following your presentation

- Individual workstations:
  - consider securing these stations by removing the taskbar to prevent students from "creative" reconfigurations of icons, files, etc.
  - consider the need to include ADA-compliant workstations with a large monitor, special keyboards, software to enlarge fonts and graphics, etc.
  - determine the space requirements per workstation (placement of the CPU, the number of students per station)
- Projection units and screen options:
  - LCD panel placed on an overhead projector and connected to the instructor's station with a cable
  - high-resolution computer projector connected directly to the computer CPU
  - test the screen with the projection unit to check how the images will appear and whether there are problems with distortions at the top, bottom, or sides of the screen
- Furniture:
  - select tables that are ergonomically designed for computer workstations
  - provide space at each workstation for students to place materials such as notebooks or manuals
  - decide upon the configuration for the instructor's station (sitting or standing; this will depend upon your teaching style)

Step 4. Design the Floor Plan

- Network connections, cabling, and electricity:
  - coordinate with your college computer department on the interface between the classroom and the college network; determine the number of ports required
  - use standard network connectors
  - bundle the cables and electrical wires neatly and systematically from the outset
  - double the number of outlets you think you will need to accommodate future growth and to create flexibility of workstation placement; the physical realities of the room will determine the placement of electrical outlets (drops from the ceiling or through the floor)
- Lighting
  - design a flexible lighting system that will enable you to brighten or dim specific areas of the room
  - if possible, use incandescent lighting, because fluorescent lights cause major problems with glare

- Temperature and ventilation:
  — if possible, try to maintain a moderate temperature in the range of 65–68 degrees for the sake of both the equipment and the humans!
- Configuration of workstations:
  — determine the kind of configuration that will best suit most of your training methods (theater, horseshoe, circle, small groupings, etc.)
  — make sure that students seated at any individual workstation will be able to see the projection screen
  — design the seating so that people can easily pass between the workstations and that you can quickly reach the stations as you assist with the hands-on training; avoid long rows with no breaks in the middle
  — incorporate ADA regulations concerning accessibility to the room and the workstations

MANAGING INSTRUCTIONAL MATERIALS

To keep a record of the course content and sessions that are taught, as well as to organize the instructional materials that are distributed, you should maintain the following electronic and/or paper files:

- a detailed outline of the presentation
- the course title and name of faculty for which the presentations were developed
- copies of the library research projects; if you developed and graded an assignment, you may want to keep copies or samples of the students' work
- a list or copies of the hand-outs you distributed to the students
- a summary of student and faculty evaluations
- the number of students attending and participating
- the names of the librarians teaching specific courses and presentations.

Other types of files to consider maintaining are:
- a database or log of search examples—it takes time to develop examples that illustrate a specific concept (such as search strategy, type of resource); maintaining a database could save you future preparation time
- a master list of frequently requested resources and databases that includes brief descriptions and search strategies you can easily

"cut and paste" when designing a customized hand-out (at one of our libraries the master list is affectionately labeled ELMER FUD—Eclectic Library of Multiple Electronic Resources and Frequently Used Databases).

If you are teaching credit courses, there will be other types of information that you have to maintain, such as class lists, grades, and other student information. You should contact the registration office or the department that handles academic affairs (be it advisors, department chairs, curriculum committee, or the like) to find out what records you are required to keep.

ANNUAL REPORTS

Writing annual reports is not a task that is enthusiastically embraced by any "normal" person. However, these reports can be very useful in presenting a strong case for additional staffing and funding, as well as in planning for the future. If you have maintained the information recommended in the previous section, however, you will find it very easy to pull together all the information you need to write your annual report.

In addition to compiling statistics for the current year, prepare a comparative analysis with previous years using a bar graph, for example, to illustrate growth and trends. Review and analyze the results of the evaluations from students and faculty and discuss with your colleagues their perceptions of your positive achievements and areas that may need improvement. This analysis will be enable you to develop goals and objectives for the next academic year. Share your annual report with your administration, especially when you (or your library director) are preparing your budget requests for the next year. Prepare and disseminate a summary of your annual report to the faculty as a way of promoting your instructional program and as feedback on the accomplishments of your collaborative teaching efforts.

KEEPING CURRENT

As librarians we understand the need to keep current with the literature and new developments within our profession and specialties. If you are relatively new to the practice and art of instruction, the following is a list of some of the major resources that you will find useful.

ASSOCIATIONS AND ORGANIZATIONS

Within the American Library Association (ALA), there are several units that are of particular relevance concerning bibliographic and information literacy instruction. To join these units, you must also become a member of ALA. For membership information you may link to ALA's Home Page (www.ala.org) or contact ALA headquarters at:

> 50 E. Huron St.
> Chicago, IL 60611
> 312–944–6780 or 800–545–2433

Listed below are some units you may wish to consider joining:

- Association of College and Research Libraries (ACRL): A division of ALA representing academic and research libraries. Produces a number of publications including professional journals (one of which is listed below) and standards and guidelines. Sponsors professional conferences (annual spring meeting and meetings in conjunction with ALA annual and mid-winter conferences). Check out the ACRL Web site for more information and links to meeting information, publications, and links to other instruction Web sites. URL: www.ala.org/acrl.html

Within ACRL are a number of sections including, the Instruction Section. The mission of this section is " . . . to enhance the ability of academic and research librarians involved in bibliographic instruction to serve effectively the library and information needs of current and potential users." www.lib.utexas.edu/is/

- Library Instruction Round Table (LIRT): The focus of this round table is "to advocate library instruction as a means for developing competent library and information use as a part of lifelong learning." Diogenes.Baylor.edu/Library/LIRT/
- National Library Orientation Exchange (LOEX): This is a clearinghouse of instructional materials and is based at the University Library of Eastern Michigan University at Ypsilanti. LOEX

also sponsors annual conferences. For more information contact:

> LOEX Clearinghouse for Libraries
> University Library
> Eastern Michigan University
> Ypsilanti, Michigan 48197
> 313–487–0168

JOURNALS

These journals are excellent resources on information literacy instruction methods and trends.

- *College and Research Libraries.* A bimonthly publication of ACRL that is included in the membership dues. Subscription cost for nonmembers is $50. Available from:
  > American Library Association
  > 50 E. Huron St.
  > Chicago, IL 60611

- *Journal of Academic Librarianship.* A bimonthly publication that includes both research and practice-oriented articles. Subscription cost is $160 ($60 for individual). Available from:
  > JAI Press
  > 55 Old Post Rd., No. 2
  > Box 1678
  > Greenwich, CT 06836-1678

- *Research Strategies.* A quarterly publication devoted to library instruction. Subscription cost is $42 ($28 for individual). Available from:
  > Mountainside Publishing
  > 321 S. Main Street, Suite 300
  > Ann Arbor, MI 48107

- *RQ.* A quarterly publication of the ALA's Reference and User Services Association, included in membership. Nonmembership subscription is $50. The focus is upon reference services, but there are a number of relevant articles addressing library instruction. Available from:
  > American Library Association
  > 50 E. Huron Street
  > Chicago, IL 60611

- *RSR: Reference Services Review*. A quarterly publication. Subscription cost is $79. Available from:
  Pierian Press
  Box 1808
  Ann Arbor, MI 48106

In addition to the library professional journals, you may want to peruse some of the publications in higher education to keep current with the issues, pedagogical methods, and trends that will affect your institution and subsequently your instructional program. Two publications that give the "big picture" are:

- *Change: The Magazine of Higher Education*. Subscription cost is $65 ($34 for individual). Available from:
  Heldref Publications
  1319 18th Street, N.W.
  Washington, D.C. 20036–1802

- *The Chronicle of Higher Education*. Subscription cost is $67.50. Available from:
  Chronicle of Higher Education
  1255 23rd St., N.W., Suite 700
  Washington, D.C. 20037

BIBLIOGRAPHIC INSTRUCTION LISTSERV

The Bibliographic Instruction listserv (BI-L) is the primary source for all sorts of issues pertaining to library instruction. It is a "must" for any librarian involved in teaching. To subscribe, send an e-mail to: listserv@listservbyu.edu.

In the body of your e-mail state: "Subscribe BL-I first name last name."

WEB SITES

There are numerous Web sites that librarians have published on their instructional services and tutorials. The following are just a very few samples to get you started.

- Bibliographic Instruction (collection of examples and resources by Bud Curnoles of the University of Maryland):
  umbc7.umbc.edu/~curnoles/bibinstr.html

- Bibliographic Resources on the Net:
  www.lib.berkeley.edu/Teaching Lib/BIRsources.html

- Library Instruction Tutorials on the LIRT Home Page: Diogenes.Baylor.edu/Library/LIRT/lirtproj.html

- Web Site on Information Literacy Resources: www.cas.usf.edu/lis/il

NOTE

1. Cheryl LaGuardia, et al. *Teaching the New Library: How-To-Do-It Manual for Planning and Designing Instructional Programs* (New York: Neal-Schuman, 1996), pp. 116–126.

SUGGESTED FURTHER READING ON DESIGNING ELECTRONIC CLASSROOMS

This chapter presented an overview of the issues and details you will need to address when designing an electronic classroom. The following resources provide more in-depth descriptions.

"Facilities Design Criteria for the Construction and Renovation of Multimedia Classrooms at Case Western Reserve University." Prepared by the Department of Audio-Visual Services. 1997. Very detailed description of the planning process and architectural design of a state-of-the-art multimedia electronic classroom. cnswww.cns.cwru.edu/tour/Tours/CWRUnet_Tours/Elect_Class_Tour/EC_Facilities_Design.html

Hinchliffe, Lisa Janicke. *Planning an Electronic Library Classroom: An Annotated Bibliography*. 1994. http://alexia.lis.uiuc.edu/~janicke/Abstracts.html

Purdue University Libraries Electronic Classroom. Includes list of the hardware and vendors, software configurations of the instructor and individual workstations, floorplan, guidelines, and policies. thorplus.lib.purdue.edu/library_info/departments/ugrl/lec/index.html

Vasi, John, and Cheryl LaGuardia. "Creating a Library Electronic Classroom." *ONLINE Magazine* 18 (5) (September/October 1994): 75–84. Describes the design of the electronic classroom at the University of California (Santa Barbara) Library.

INDEX

ABOUT THE AUTHORS

Rosemary Young and Stephena Harmony are faculty librarians at the University of Cincinnati. Young has been the head librarian at the Timothy C. Day Technical Library, Ohio Mechanics Institute/OMI, College of Applied Science, since 1985. She has extensive experience in developing and providing information literacy instruction and library orientations in the undergraduate environment from freshman English through senior-level engineering design courses. She created a three-credit-hour general education course on information literacy. Young is the co-author of *Moving and Reorganizing a Library* with Marianna Wells, published in 1997 by Gower Publishing Limited. She also was a scriptwriter for the video *Searching UCLID and OhioLINK*, produced in 1996. She received her master's of library science from the University of Kentucky College of Library and Information Science in 1984.

Stephena Harmony has been the director of the Library/Media Services Department at the Raymond Walters College (RWC) since 1994. Her previous positions include the head of information services at the Health Sciences Library of the University of Cincinnati and head librarian at the Cincinnati EPA Library. Her experience in library instruction programming includes designing presentations for both undergraduate and graduate students. She is also the program director for the RWC Library Technology associate degree and professional certificate program. Harmony was the executive producer and scriptwriter for the video *Searching UCLID and OhioLINK*. In 1976 she received her master's in library science from the Case Western Reserve University School of Library Science.